# Drug Preventic
# Just Say

# Drug Prevention - Just Say Now

Peter Stoker

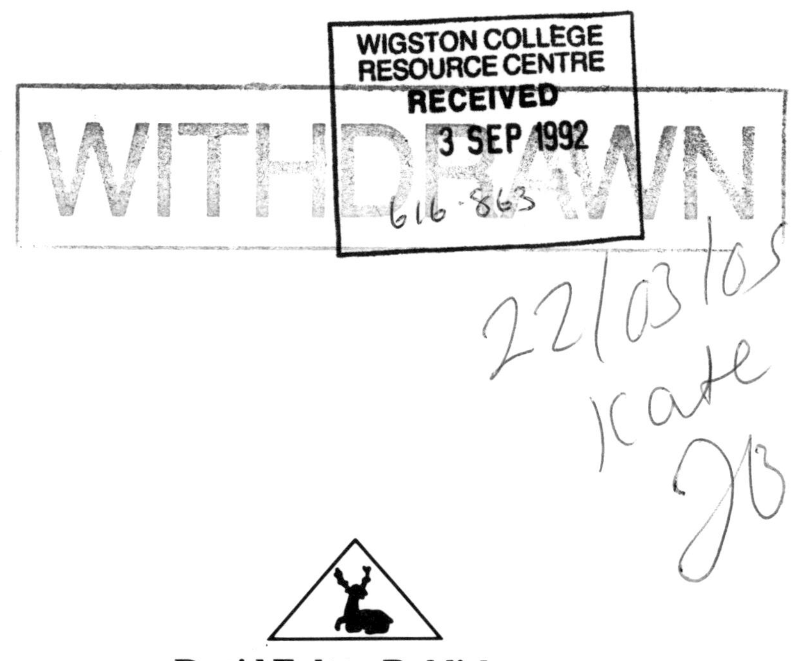


**David Fulton Publishers**
London

David Fulton Publishers Ltd
2 Barbon Close, London WC1N 3JX

First published in Great Britain by
David Fulton Publishers 1992

Note: The right of the author to be identified as the author of this work has been asserted by him in accordance with the Copyright, Designs and Patents Act 1988



*British Library Cataloguing in Publication Data*

A catalogue record for this book is
available from the British Library

ISBN 1-85346-235-7



Typeset by Tony Hibbett, London
Printed in Great Britain by BPCC Wheaton Ltd

# CONTENTS 

**ACKNOWLEDGEMENTS**
**FOREWORD**
**INTRODUCTION**

**DEVELOPMENT OF THE TECHNOLOGY**

1. **What is Prevention?**
   The backdrop; where Prevention fits in. Obstacles to Prevention. History lesson. Does it work? The idea whose time has come. Europe est arrivée.
2. **The Current Drug/Alcohol Scene in Britain**
   Substances update. Professional responses. Alcohol - a special case.
3. **The Legislation Movement**
4. **Learning from the World**
   Where to start. America: north, south, east and west. The EAP in Business. Australia -caravans and kangaroos. Australasia unlimited. Europe galvanised.
5. **The British Experience**
   Historical perspective. British responses to drug use. The dawn of Health. Specific projects: Teenex, Fast Forward, Youth to Youth, Youthlink.
6. **Bringing it All Together**
   Why use drugs? True Prevention, and its relation to Whole Health. Characteristics of Effective Prevention.

**APPLICATION OF THE TECHNOLOGY**

7. **A Model Prevention Strategy**
Burn out and how to do it. Where to look for help. Communication near and far.

8. **Process and Programme Specifics**
A model timetable for primary and secondary schools. Peer education. Evaluating materials, programmes, video/film.

9. **Teacher Power**
The teaching scene. Attainment targets for Prevention.

10. **Peer Power**
Peer education. Evaluations. British examples.

11. **Parent Power**
An untapped resource in Britain. Some useful reading. The first steps.

12. **Community Power**
A role for everyone. Businesses. Sportspersons. The Legal Fraternity. Newshounds. Prayer Power. Medical Muscle. Altogether now.

**Epilogue**

**Appendix A** - Recommended reading list, chapter-by-chapter, and contact addresses.

**Appendix B** - Cannabis, the Insidious Growth.

## ACKNOWLEDGEMENTS

To the production team, coming first for a change: Debs Creedy, Wendy Walker, Carol Faulkner and Maureen Tucker on wordprocessors, and Tony Hibbett, typesetting and layout. Deep gratitude to you all. (P.S. The cheque is in the post.)

To Bill Rice, for inspiration and support over many years, and for the same reasons to Buddy Gleaton, Lisa Ellsworth, Kay Bondurant, Durand Farley and many more at PRIDE. To Lynne Kauffman, for an Education Adviser's eye view. To Barbara Dean, for Families Together, a great concept. To Lois Collins, Sandy/Mandy/Andy, Joe and John... y'all showed me what Clayton County can be proud of, and to Barbara and Ed Toningsen for bringing TRIBES to Britain.

To Roy Evans who gave me the vital start with this book and David Fulton who made sure I finished it. And, between these mileposts, Eddie Ishag of Business Against Drugs and the Home Office CDPU for their invaluable support.

To the Teenex Gang, young and old, past and present, who constantly demonstrate that primary prevention is alive and well. And to the Portugese and Panamanian adoptive parents of Teenex.

To Ann, my wife, (very) professional colleague, friend and energiser. To my parents, who gave me my drive. And to my daughter Emma, for faith in the future.

## SUPPORT

The production of this book was made possible by the physical and moral support of Business Against Drugs and the Home Office Central Drug Prevention Unit, to whom grateful thanks are offered.

# FOREWORD

Some time ago I read with interest an article arguing the case for continued commitment to primary prevention. It was the rarity of such an article that caught my eye; the greater space being given to other strategies could mislead one to believe that prevention has little to say. The truth is very different. I believe this book gives you that truth.

The author of the article that originally caught my attention, Peter Stoker, has developed and expanded his case in this his most recent work. I welcome the review of evidence relating to the viability of prevention strategies. It is also particularly pleasing to have, among other benefits, a clearly-argued point of view concerning ways in which prevention and harm reduction might beneficially co-exist.

As someone with a long-time interest in and commitment to the principle of prevention, I have been dismayed by those who have promoted the idea that with primary prevention and harm reduction it has to be an "either/or" situation. I do not accept this. Simple observation of what actually goes on in the drug field clearly shows that both strategies are in use. As a seasoned counsellor and advocate with drug/alcohol users as well as a prevention educator/trainer Peter Stoker is ideally placed to understand that. What can be said is that both strategies are not always used in appropriate circumstances.

The author's strong commitment to helping young people realise their potential through a life free of drug abuse comes through loud and clear. Some readers may find this challenge daunting, but by the end of the book no one should be left complacent.

I warmly recommend it to you.

Bill Rice
Executive Director, East Dorset Drug and Alcohol Advisory Service
Former Chief Executive Officer, TACADE.

# INTRODUCTION

Writing on this subject means keeping the eraser handy. Enthusiastically adding or changing sections to reflect new developments has been a daily task. On just one day, while driving "finished" copy to the typesetter, the radio announced "Acting Against Drug Abuse", a Health Department initiative using drama, and a major new shock-horror campaign about Solvent Abuse; meanwhile the Thought for the Day was "Prevent us, O Lord, in all we do" and how this didn't mean "hinder us", it meant "come before us"... (and keep us straight).

But then, any drug prevention worker could have told you that.

Prevention, meaning primary prevention of drugs, meaning primary prevention of all drugs of abuse (including alcohol and other legal substances), meaning encouragement, facilitation and reinforcement of a drug-free lifestyle, meaning... meaning maybe you're already lost in a maze! This book tries to guide you through that maze, with what is hopefully just enough information for the would-be prevention practitioner of whatever discipline to start useful work. And don't be shy; everyone can help.

Each chapter's subject could generate a book or two on its own. Has, in fact, as the recommended reading list in Appendix A shows. What is given here is the skeletal structure around which can be developed a model strategy for Britain. (Or indeed for other countries.)

A perennial of drug/alcohol work in Britain (and elsewhere) has been a fierce debate between advocates of primary prevention and those favouring harm reduction, for a variety of reasons. In truth we have more commonality than differences. Both strategies are Behavioural Modification attempts, and as such are difficult to achieve and evaluate as to outcome, though both can show "process" achievements. Most importantly, both are needed, as part of a "Continuum of Care", and anyone who puts people before ideology must eventually conclude this. Both, in their way, are caring policies, and neither can claim monopoly of the moral high ground.

The journalistic and political relish for "War on Drugs" rhetoric does none of us any good, implying as it does an "armed forces" campaign that will achieve a result in a finite period. A better metaphor might concern Coastal Engineering, such as the Dutch, or East Anglians, pursue. The intention is to keep the sea out, sometimes even to reclaim land lost before; if there is a breach of the wall, assertive action minimises the damage. But this action is permanent. The sea will always be with us. And let us not forget that when sea defences are under threat, the civilians - you and me - are at least as useful as the uniformed agencies in protecting what is important.

Some of the antipathy towards primary prevention comes from those who believe it to be unworkable; evidence herein should change their minds. Others are pursuing a more political agenda, with minds not interested in objective appraisal; Chapter 1.3 should inform you on this.

If this book encourages you into community action, whatever your community (school, business, neighbourhood) is, it will have achieved its primary objective. If it encourages you to make links with, or better still make visits to the projects at home and abroad and see for yourself, as I have done, this will be a bonus. If it does nothing more than provoke you into publishing a better book on the subject, then prevention will gain!

A "liberal" is described as one who is in favour of liberty and progress, is broad-minded and is in favour of empowered people realising their potential. In this context I dedicate this book to the true liberals: prevention workers everywhere.

Peter Stoker
May 1992.

# CHAPTER 1

# WHAT IS PREVENTION?

There are few subjects which generate more emotion than drugs. Even seasoned professionals in the field find themselves from time to time having driven into a cul-de-sac. Self-styled experts appear from behind every tree, delivering arguments that generate more heat than light. Teachers are sick and tired of taking the whole blame for this and indeed every other aspect of pupils' behaviour. The emergence of HIV/AIDS has added another frightening perspective. Meanwhile, Mr Suburb, bewildered and powerless in the face of an apparently unstoppable tide of teenage excess, seeks solace in another cigarette and a glass of the amber nectar, while upstairs Mrs Suburb reaches for the tranquilliser bottle...

Responses to abuse of drugs - and throughout this book that term will be taken to include the abuse of alcohol - have been attempted for as long as the drugs themselves have existed. Sometimes these have erred on the side of severity, sometimes they are so limp as to be meaningless. Many have been the inconsistencies in relation to different drugs; what some observers call the "Our Drugs and Theirs" syndrome. So, for example, legal status continues for tobacco (100,000 deaths a year) and alcohol (25,000 deaths a year) while £millions have been received by advertising agencies producing dramatic attacks on the use of heroin (200 deaths a year). At the same time, several other damaging drugs receive no preventive media exposure whatsover.

The attitude by Britain has not been without ambivalence. Compare for example the generally disapproving attitude to use of opiates by Britons in Britain with the opium monopoly in India after Clive defeated the Great Mogul in 1757, and the Opium Wars of the 19th Century in which the Chinese failed to eject Europeans promoting unrestricted use of opium which the British and others wished to aggressively market. A more modern example of this kind of double standard concerns tobacco. Manufacturers manoeuvered into displaying health warnings on their UK products, even to contemplate a ban on all advertising, are pressing ahead with power selling to all, including the young, in Third World countries. Often high tar products frowned upon here are unloaded there. What though is the relevance of all this to Prevention? Surely Prevention means Just Saying No? Far from it. For prevention to work fully it has to permeate every section of society, to challenge the attitudes and behaviour of all of us. Not just teachers but also manufacturers, media people and police, health workers and sportspersons, priests and youth workers, partners, parents and peers. But (as the music hall man said) **chiefly yourselves**.

**Where does Primary Prevention Fit In?**

Prevention is however only one of several valid responses to the abuse of drugs, which in chronological order comprise:-

Prevention -
Encouraging continuance of a drug- free lifestyle.

Harm Reduction
Identifying and encouraging least risky methods of use of specific drugs, for those unwilling to cease their use (yet, or ever).

Self-Help -
Most obviously the "Twelve Step" bodies (AA,NA,Alateen etc) but other more recent groups such as Tranx and Drinkwatch, aimed at giving strength through sharing experiences between users or people around the user.

Primary Health Care -
Clinic/hospital care for casualties either from ingestion of drugs or from accidents whilst under the influence.

Detoxification -
Either in-patient or out-patient removal of toxins incapacitating the user.

Rehabilitation -
Therapeutic communities (usually residential) aimed at allowing an ex-user to learn how to live a mature and fulfilling life without drugs.

After-Care -
Supporting ex-users to stay "dry/clean".

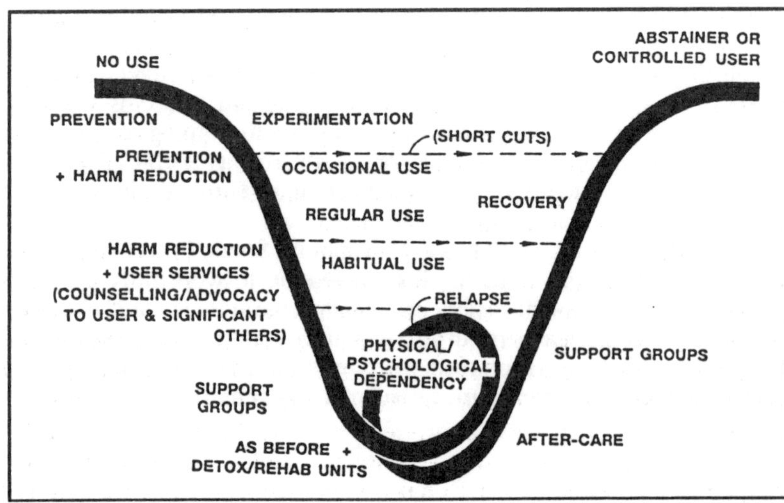


**Figure 1.1 Spectrum of drug use and responses**

There are other important responses too. The legislative and the legal systems, including the police forces who have a valuable role in prevention as well as penal action. In truth, all of society has a role to play at one stage or another.

Semantics is the "staff of life" in drug work, especially if there is funding money to be had, or if a shift in jargon can make the activity sound more positive; like the economists who refer to some Third World countries having "negative reserves". Thus, Harm Reduction is sometimes reclassified as Secondary Prevention (preventing harm) and Detoxification/Rehabilitation becomes Tertiary Prevention (preventing recurrence). This book is principally concerned with Primary Prevention, that is staying drug-free.

Then one has to define what "drug-free" means. If we use aspirin or drink coffee, we are not drug-free. What the term is commonly accepted to mean is drug-abuse-free, where abuse means "use of any illegal drug or misuse of any legal substance as a drug". (This allows for glues and solvents which are not clinically defined as drugs but are being used as such.)

Harm Reduction generates strong emotions in some quarters; isn't this just coaching young people into the use of drugs? The answer might be yes if one were to pro-actively circulate information on drug use methods to all children. This is not the way most authorities work; information on more risky and less risky drug use methods is generally confined to youth known to be (or thought to be at risk of) using and **should be accompanied by a Prevention message** (i.e. "There is no safe way to use drugs; the best way to reduce the risks of doing drugs is don't do them"). Russell Newcombe, giving harm reduction advice about Ecstasy in the Mersey Drugs Journal in 1988 says **"Zero risk from MDMA (Ecstasy) can only be achieved by not taking it."**

As an example, which puts Harm Reduction in perspective, the Health Education Authority issues recommended limits for alcohol consumption (21 units per week for a man, 14 for a woman, spread your consumption, have three or four dry days). This is Harm Reduction in the face of refusal of millions to be abstinent. One might observe that there is an absence of any Prevention message in this instance, and therefore youth is being given a tacit signal that drinking alcohol is OK. One's observation would be spot on target, and certainly the drinks industry would argue that moderate drinking is desirable for you (and them).

This is an issue deserving much more public discussion than it has had so far. A key factor in any such discussion would be defining the use of alcohol as a "beverage" or as a "drug" and at what consumption level it moves from beverage to drug (of course a transition rather than a firm boundary). It was salutory in this context to hear a French health minister on Radio 4 news in the summer of 1991, describing the new awareness in his country. Given that France is often held up as the acme of responsible drinking by the young, it was very instructive to hear his surprise and despair as he exclaimed that "French youth are now using alcohol as a drug".

One effect of the Health Authority limits is to bring the specified consumption down towards "beverage" levels for adults rather than consumption of "alcohol as a drug". The important omission in any of this is what is a responsible level of consumption for adolescents? Some groups state flatly that the consumption level for youth is "zero; there is no such thing as responsible use of alcohol by teens" (see Figure 8.2). Others argue that teaching youth to use alcohol moderately is a protection against future problem use - however, would the same argument apply to heroin? Discuss.

## Obstacles to Prevention

This convoluted complex of attitudes and values, national policies and individual behaviour bedevils any attempt to bring about a change in behaviour. Sometimes the requirements for bringing about change seem so unattainable as to be preposterous - viz, if people do drugs to escape reality, then the solution is to improve reality. Simple enough! Totally unreasonable, say others, but before you join the fatalists, the would-be preventionist can gain strength from a philosophical statement by George Bernard Shaw:-

> "The reasonable man adapts himself to the world; the unreasonable man persists in trying to adapt the world to himself. Therefore, all progress depends on the unreasonable man".

Unreasonable men, or persons, do however suffer from a perennial tendency to pull in different directions. What results is a kind of multiple tug-of-war, a net of ropes with the handkerchief (representing you and me) at the junction (see figure 1.2 below). The handkerchief whisks back, forth and sideways, with the Government endeavouring to judge who has won (and therefore which laws to make/repeal/amend). Not easy. This is explored in more detail in Chapter 3.

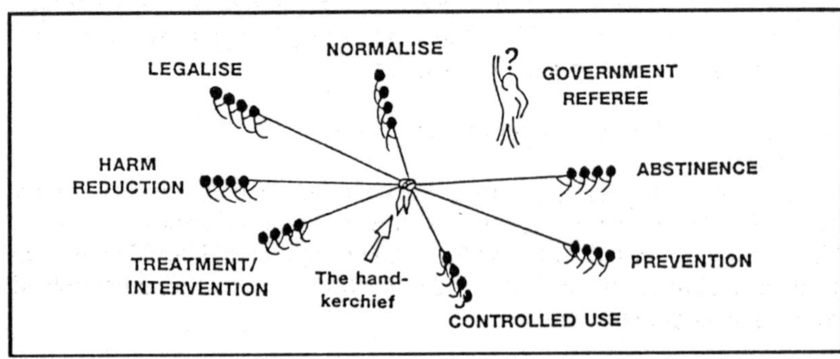


**Figure 1.2 The Drug Tug of War**

Against this blurred and shifting backdrop it is important to understand how prevention has evolved, why it is as it is today. "Prevention", the term used by the profession for decades, has unfortunate overtones of patriarchy, of mandatory instruction. The dictionary does not altogether help, in defining prevention as "to obstruct, to hinder". For the true intention of the word in the context of this work one must go back to the latin root "praevenire" meaning simply "to come before". To get in early. This is the essence of prevention but as has been found, for example, with smoking prevention it is necessary to not only get in early but to keep going; the effect does wear off.

## The History of Prevention

Development of prevention technology into its present sophisticated state has been a semi-empirical process. Techniques and materials have been developed continuously since the 1950s, some being shelved because of their limited effect but others being absorbed into the panoply of responses to drug abuse. A potted history might run as follows. The unbracketed decades are for America; the bracketed are for Britain,:-

1950s/60s **Scare Tactics**
(1970s)
"Do this drug and you'll be doomed". Lurid pictures of dead bodies or damaged lungs, livers etc. This technique floundered because youth knew others who had used these drugs and not suffered such a fate (even if some others unknown to these youth had). They therefore rejected everything the teacher said, destroying all credibility. Some youth were even attracted by the lurid stories and saw this behaviour as a new and exciting statement of their individuality.

1970s **Values and Feelings**
(1970s/80s)
Teachers attempted to draw out value clarification within the class, to seek consensus on values beneficial to society. Useful in itself, this technique often shied away from specific information and consequences of drug use, and therefore had little impact in this sphere.

(1980s **Alternatives and Decisions**
(1980s)
A strong push to divert youth from negative to positive took place. Recreational activities were promoted and presented as "drug-free" events. This technique was coupled with detailed experiential involvement in decision-making and the skills needed for this. The two together helped youth to make positive choices.

Early 1980s **Refusal Skills**
(Late 1980s)
The birth of "Just Say No". Schools taught youth refusal skills, in part using role-play to explore and reinforce this. This was a valuable learning experience for both pupils and teachers, as the power of peer pressure became more apparent.

1980s **Community Involvement**
(Late 1980s/90s)
At last spreading beyond the confines of the classroom, the prevention movement formed coalitions between community bodies and educational establishments. The birth of the Parents movement. This was in part due to a greater recognition of the effect of overall environment (not just school environment) on behaviour. The "non-use norm" started to be promoted, viz the recognition that, despite media scares etc., the majority of youth are non-users.

1990s **Systems Approach**
(Not yet)
An integrated approach emerges, interrelating and co-ordinating school, family, workplace, etc., in a rational model based on study of how the components of a community interact. Defining and encouraging each to play their part.

**So Does it Work?**
Yes.

Next question?

**How do you Know it Works?**

This is not as easy to demonstrate as might first appear. It is not simply a matter of instantaneously measuring changes in behaviour i.e. are fewer people using drugs after our prevention campaign than before it? There may be several reasons which have brought about such a change of behaviour. The subject may indeed have been influenced by the prevention campaign. They may however have been affected by extraneous factors, changes in their life, for example. The change may be no more than faddish, because the topic is in the news, but such a change may not last. And lastly, the subject may simply have changed their mind, without reference to the prevention work.

This inherent difficulty in evaluation of behavioural change is well understood by academics, (but this evinces no sympathy from the Legalisation tug-of-war team). Academically rigorous evaluations demonstrating successful prevention are few in number, not only because of these technological difficulties but also because of cost limitations. If there is only a small amount of money available for the project then evaluation is often the first casualty.

Confirmation that prevention does work can be illustrated by, amongst others, the following bodies of evidence. In West Germany as long ago as 1980 use of peer groups was shown to have helped prevent youth drug use. One of the best documented prevention projects concerns the Bowling Green Community in Western Kentucky. That such a high level of academic rigour has been and still is being sustained is due in no small part to Dr Ronald Adams of the University of Western Kentucky. Ron designed and supervises the PRIDE (Parents Resource Institute for Drug Education) Questionnaire, which annually and confidentially questions thousands of young people across America about their drug use habits. In Bowling Green this questionnaire has been sustained annually since 1984 and has been correlated with an enthusiastic community prevention programme involving schools, parents, businesses, churches, sports/social clubs, police, social services, etc. From the start of the prevention programme there has been a steady decline in use of all substances, in contrast with the increase in use seen in America generally. The cost of sustaining this programme has been tiny in comparison to some government-initiated campaigns; in Cost Benefit Analysis terms the Bowling Green programme shows major return on investment. Chapter 4 gives more detail on PRIDE and Bowling Green.

Almost 2000 miles to the west of Kentucky lies Oakland, California, notorious in recent times for its tough environment. A few miles away is the Center for Human Development which since 1974 has addressed the particular subject of drug abuse and how to prevent it. Incentive to succeed came in part from the heroin addiction suffered by the founder's son.

Observations of school environment led to the development of a process called TRIBES (meaning small families). TRIBES uses co-operative learning and social development techniques which have been found to not only help prevent drug abuse but also prevent other negative behaviour (such as racism, bullying, truancy) and also yield two big plusses - less teacher burn-out/drop-out, and improved academic performance.

Should you need any more convincing that prevention can do the job, the National Household Survey for the whole of the USA ought to do the trick. Conducted bienially, these surveys have for years been showing a serious growth in usage of all types of drug. In 1986 the first light appeared in the gloom, when usage of cannabis started to peak off; however, use of all other drugs continued to rise. Four years later, in 1990, the real dividend started to appear with a substantial downturn in the use of all substances. Some elements such as cocaine use by high school seniors showed a massive 50% drop from figures two years previously.

No one can deny the pro-drug lobby have fancy footwork, even when pinned down by facts like these. When the Household survey was showing growth of use it was held up as an example of the failure of prevention (and of the War on Drugs). Now that it shows decline in use it is described as biased; citizens are said to be falsifying their survey questionnaires in the face of "Just Say No" fervour. You, the reader must be left to draw your own conclusions about **that**.

Police and Customs officials, amongst others, readily acknowledge that their own efforts affect only a small percentage of people actually involved in drugs, and their dissuading effect is also small (but valuable). In a selfless analysis they universally conclude that prevention is the answer. From this the consensus is that the downturn in use evidenced by the National Household Survey is due to prevention, and a lot of it. America has been working hard at prevention for nearly fifteen years. We should be aware therefore that Britain will not turn its similar usage growth curves into decline without at least similar effort.

## An Idea Whose Time has Come

When you find the tackling is getting tougher, that's a fair indication you're getting close to goal. The pro-drug campaigners and the compulsive sceptics are scorning the latest (1990) National Biennial Household Survey results in the USA, implying that this is nothing less than a conspiracy by the American public to make prevention workers feel good. Prevention workers have every right to feel good, for the Household results make it clear that prevention **is** possible and sustainable. Goals are being achieved.

Meanwhile, on this side of the Atlantic, there are signs of new growth in many countries. In Britain there has been in recent years a slow but steady increase in interest in prevention. In 1988 the author was sent by the Foreign and Commonwealth Office to the PRIDE International Drugs Conference as their official observer. Copies of the author's report were sent to the Home Office, Departments of Health/Education and to the All-Party Parliamentary Committee on Drug Misuse (Chaired by Tim Rathbone, MP). The following March saw the Ministerial Summit featuring Margaret Thatcher and Perez de Cuellar; not quite the "prevention conference" that had been mooted after the PRIDE Conference, but it did spark into life two new enterprises. The Home Office-based Central Drugs Prevention Unit was given a budget of £7.5m in its first two years, and at least a three year life to fund local prevention units in up to thirty areas considered most needy. The Department of Health-based Demand Reduction Task Force is charged with distributing current expertise on demand reduction around the world. In order to become a nett exporter of expertise the Task Force will have to absorb and catalogue a vast array of knowledge in other countries, and this should make it a very valuable adjunct to prevention efforts in this country.

At a more local level there are pockets of good practice; these can remain unknown nationally for some time, as the programme workers concentrate on their local task, leaving dissemination for another day. A recent chance to exchange experiences in the British Isles and Eire took place in February 1991 in Wales. Conference delegates participated in rotation in workshops organised by four projects:-

| | |
|---|---|
| Fast Forward - (Scotland) | Established by the Scottish Association of Youth Clubs in 1987. |
| Youthlink - (Wales) | Born out of youth participation from 1985 to 1987 by the Council for Wales for Voluntary Services. |
| Youth to Youth - (Eire) | Formed by the Catholic Social Services Centre in Dublin in 1984. |
| Teenex - (England) | Written by the author's professional colleage and wife, after UK and overseas research. Launched 1988. |

Chapter 5 gives extended information on all these projects.

**Europe Catches Up**

For many years Europe too has had its isolated pockets of good practice. It has also had a wall across it, hampering even the most willing disseminator. A few Europeans and Scandinavians sometimes made it to PRIDE conferences but the showing was slight. The full extent of Europe's increasing commitment first became clear at a small gathering in Belgium in October 1991. Delegates came from both sides of the wall, from East Germany, Hungary, Poland, Luxembourg, France, West Germany, the three Belgiums (French, Flemish, German), Portugal, England and - quirkily - Quebec, a kind of honorary European country! EC Representatives were there in strength.

Two firm resolutions were passed. To hold a major conference in Belgium in May 1992, and to form a European Association for Primary Prevention. A Steering Committee has been formed.

The synthesis of all these fresh initiatives, in Britain and Europe, is that Prevention is being recognised as a viable and valuable initiative in response to drug use, and a pre-emptive one at that. Counselling, treating and generally discouraging drug users will continue to play a part in the total response. For Prevention however, the idea whose time has come, one can truly Just Say Now.

## CHAPTER 2

# THE CURRENT DRUG/ALCOHOL SCENE IN BRITAIN

The lay observer is largely at the mercy of the media who have a free hand in determining what is newsworthy, plus any "hearsay" he or she may pick up from social discourse. Thus, in late 1989 we were about to be overwhelmed with Crack which would prove addictive at the first hit. And of course solvents have gone away, heroin is no longer a big deal, and Ecstasy and Acid are not now available at dance parties.

If you believe all that, you are the kind of reader the papers are looking for.

A general professional consensus of the situation in 1992 might go something like this:

**Cannabis** Estimated to be used by between 2-3,000,000 people in Britain (and therefore **not** used by 54,000,000). The most common illegal drug featured in arrest statistics, increasingly receiving a caution on first arrest. Strength of cannabis much higher than the "flower-power 60s". Now known to be physically harmful. Cannabis dependency and psychosis now identified. **Please read Appendix B.**

**Alcohol** With tobacco, is the drug most used by adolescents. Costs British business around £2000 million per year. Costs British families about 25,000-40,000 deaths per year. Equivocal attitudes to use as "beverage" rather than "drug" blur the issues in relation to drinking by adolescents, equivocation which the drinks industry does little to counter. The law on alcohol has the same age-limit quirkiness as for tobacco, viz at a given age it is not illegal for a youth to have and consume but it is illegal for someone to sell it to them.

**Tobacco** The third (with alcohol and cannabis) of the "gateway" drugs i.e. substances which those now using harder drugs once started with. Surveys by MORI (1990) showed that 50% of tobacco smokers had also tried an illegal drug compared with only 2% of non-smokers. (This finding has been repeated in other countries.) Is likely to cost Marlboro a packet; Marlboro Man is suing them, having contracted lung cancer. Earlier health campaigns were successful in reducing smoking prevalence but there are fresh signs of resurgence, especially amongst young girls. Research in China shows a link between smoking and cervical cancer.

**Amphetamine** Continues to be used by sizeable numbers although its popularity has been partly offset by the promotion of Ecstasy and LSD (Acid) around "Raves" (dance parties). Psychosis in withdrawal is of concern and has produced suicides. Paranoia is common.

**LSD (Acid)** Arguably the most powerful common street drug; a microdot is all it takes, then "newspaper taxis appear on the shore". Makes a yearly appearance in the gullible press pages, around Halloween, when fake police/hospital notices arrive, talking about Blue Stars transfers found by young children, absorbed through the skin and causing death. There are no recorded deaths from ingestion, but cases have been seen of latent schizophrenia being brought out (to full-blown) by users of LSD.

**Ecstasy** House parties are deemed to have gone respectable by becoming Raves, now in legal sites with police/local authority licensing. Drugs are, as you might expect, still there and you don't have to look very hard to see them. Ecstasy is starting to appear in the presenting problems of clients; it is in part an amphetamine and as such it can be expected to produce similar physiological effects. There were 6 deaths attributed to E ingestion in 1990, from "Neuroleptic Malignant Syndrome". New-found harmony on the football terraces is credited to several measures; police have observed that many fans are still stoned from the previous night's Rave. Some new nicknames on the street; "Biscuits", "White Calis", "California Sunrise", "Love Doves".

**Heroin** The number of (Home Office) registered users continues to climb whilst still being only a fraction of the actual users. Chasing (inhaling fumes from heroin powder liquefied over a flame) is currently the more prevalent practice because of concern over injection risks (abcesses, hepatitis, HIV). Some locations such as Liverpool have higher prevalence of injecting users.

**Cocaine** Seems to stay mainly confined to certain areas such as Inner London. Cost puts it out of the reach of many young people.

**Crack** Home Office now believe there is a racial bias in the user population, more black youth than white use in inner city areas such as Brixton. Swift onset of dependency is plausible because users often rapidly repeat use to escape the deep "crash" which follows the rapid but short-lived high. Scotland Yard Crack Squads have dispersed since the influx (predicted by New York DEA senior officer Bob Stuttmann to appalled British Chief Constables in April 1989) failed to happen, but the Cry Wolf syndrome is not to be overlooked; Canada now has a sizeable crack problem because it dismantled too much of its resources when it experienced false alarms some years ago.

**Solvents** Continue to kill substantial numbers of people, 100-200 per year, and victims tend to be young; some, but not all, are first time users. Deaths from the toxic effect of the substances are now a much higher proportion of total deaths (including accidential consequences) compared to the early days of glue sniffing. This means that even sniffers who have some experience are now at greater risks. The butane can is today's essential accessory. Recent reports have referred to youth breaking open neon striplights and snorting the powder inside - the precise effects are as yet unknown.

**Tranquillisers** Not generally a youth problem by the time it does become a problem (though the author has dealt with clients who started using at age 14). There are still thousands of sufferers needing treatment, counselling and therapy. Though this form of drug dependency differs from the others in that drugs were mostly prescribed rather than self- obtained, there are similarities in reasons for starting and/or continuing, which can include stress, grief, anxiety and a wish to escape. For this reason prevention has a part to play, offering a drug-free route to dealing with these conditions.

**Steroids** One of the several types of sports drug abuse, most commonly related to muscle/weight gain. Almost epidemic amongst weightlifters. Deaths have resulted. Recent Scotland Yard Forensic Department research has linked sexual abuse to some steroid abusers.

**Toad Licking** An exotic, if not revolting way of achieving "heightened consciousness", using a dumb creature. Can be risky; it is poisonous. Mainly confined to North America and Australia.

**Nootropics** So-called "mind-improving" drugs. Still largely unexplored territory. Like anything affecting the Central Nervous System, dependency is just one of the risks.

**Tomorrow's World - Electronic Drugs**

Forget Nintendo!* Not generally recognised (yet) as a drug, Virtual Reality could be a real problem in the future. Sophisticated hardware and software allows the user to disappear into another world without the use of pills, powders or fluids; no injection needed; nothing illegal. The cost will drop as with all computer products, especially where it is provided in amusement arcades. The form of habituation will be somewhere between the gaming machine addict and the drug dependent. Brave new world.

* On second thoughts, don't forget Nintendo. The Professional Association of Teachers have warned parents to watch for Nintendo addiction symptoms; "Lack of speech, little sign of life, total absence of thought" (i.e. 95% of all pupils). Impatience for satisfaction accompanied by aggression; "Me Feel Good Now" is another worrying consequence.

## Professional Response Fashions

Professionals as a species are not faddish. Generally they prefer to provide their services in a steady manner along a clear route without sudden changes of direction. However, from time to time substantial shifts of attitude are induced, either by conditions in the working environment or by the persuasive arguments of new theories (or old theories in new clothes).

Drugs professionals are however more vulnerable than many because of the volatile nature of the drug environment, the high emotions generated, the high pressure arguments that are constructed in favour of very diverse "solutions" and because of the absence so far (and probably for ever) of an ultimate panacea.

The evolution of prevention into its present form has been described in Chapter 1, and the lag behind the USA and others has been illustrated. To gain a full picture of the situation with drugs professionals it is necessary to consider recent history both in the intervention (counselling and treatment) sector and in the education (occasionally including prevention) sector.

Intervention workers have had to face and somehow cope with a substantial increase in prevalence of "traditional" British drugs, the emergence of problematic use of "new" drugs, and at best no increase in resources; sometimes retrenchment. Extra to this has come an order of magnitude increase in the problems associated with injecting drug use (traditionally abcesses and hepatitis) - that is, HIV and AIDS. Whilst HIV has fundamentally changed emphasis, with concentration on injecting drug use, it is worth remembering that drug workers have always addressed the subject of risky behaviour whilst under the influence of any drug, injectable or not. HIV is not the only sexually-transmissible disease which intervention workers have to confront, and caution in sexual behaviour has always been in the drug worker's repertoire of advice.

**It is worth positing, to bring home to the multitude of young people who believe themselves out of the danger zone, that the most 'dangerous' drug for transmission of HIV may well not be heroin, or indeed any injectable drug, but may in fact be alcohol; this because very many more take a chance on unprotected sex when influenced by alcohol, compared to the numbers "jacking up".**

The argument has been advanced that HIV/AIDS is "a bigger threat to society than drugs". This statement has more than a pinch of validity to it, provided one defines what that threat is. HIV certainly concerns the whole of society, not solely gays and drug users (and members of the gay and the drug using community would certainly include many people whose impairment or death would be a severe setback to society; beware stereotypes!). The threat may then be considered as disablement and/or loss of significant numbers of the population, plus fear-paralysis and grief- impairment of many more. Certainly a huge threat.

But the onset of this threat does not remove the threats which drug use continues to pose to society, threats on which delivery is regularly made. The appropriate response therefore is one in which priorities and resources are determined locally (for conditions will vary greatly with regions) in line with regional and national policy.

This is not always happening in intervention work because of three factors; a lack of perspective at government level over relative funding for HIV work in comparison with drugs work; a sanguine approach towards some drugs at the spuriously-termed "soft" end of the scale; and finally because of the acceptance by some workers of the arguments put forward by the drug "liberalisation" lobby. These last two factors stem in part from the tendency of drug workers to "go more than half way" in developing rapport with their clients, a temptation to which the author can testify. At its most extreme it becomes over-identification, which for example in Switzerland led the cadre of workers appointed for outreach and prevention to transform themselves into a pressure group for drug legalisation!

On the other side of this coin, outreach harm reduction workers in Norway also promote primary prevention and see no dichotomy between the two types of activity. According to these workers, such a split is more apparent than real; it is perfectly possible to say to a user that your preference is that people in general don't use, but you will accept a user as he/she is and work with them to achieve whatever they want to achieve. This may indeed be abstinence but may instead relate to bringing existing chaotic use under control, or simply giving guidance about the existing pattern and level of use. The way the drug worker establishes a relationship with the user should be capable of overcoming any apparent inconsistency that clients may perceive; for intervention drug workers to buy into the suggestion that such a dichotomy exists produces an unnecessary and counterproductive schism between intervention and prevention.

## The Influence of Alcohol

Considering those drug and alcohol workers involved in prevention, one first needs to refer to the three definitions - primary/secondary/tertiary prevention - in Chapter 1. In the alcohol field people will introduce themselves as "prevention workers" but what they actually do is harm reduction (i.e. secondary prevention) by educating about "responsible drinking". This contrasts with the attitude of American primary prevention workers who say that for an adolescent there is no such thing as responsible drinking and to support this they point to studies showing greater impact of alcohol on growing bodies, earlier onset of alcoholism, and the greater propensity for those who drink (or smoke) to progress to illegal drugs.

One should not overlook the differences in laws between America and Britain, for in many US states drinking under 21 is illegal, whether at home or not. Under British law it is not actually illegal for the young, even as young as 5, to consume alcohol at home, only to buy it, have it bought for them, or consume it in a public place.

Alcohol confuses more than the consumer, therefore. It confuses professionals who have to work with both the consumers and the non-consumers. If alcohol (and likewise tobacco) were to be invented today they would both be scheduled as Class A drugs and declared illegal. Because alcohol has been legal in many countries for thousands of years, any attempts to make it illegal would meet the same response as Prohibition in America. That is, notwithstanding the fact that Prohibition did in fact succeed in reducing alcoholism and (can you believe?) alcohol-related crime, the majority public attitude was in favour of keeping alcohol legal. This is one important distinction between alcohol and cannabis; the latter has been generally illegal worldwide for thousands of years, and majority public attitude is against legalisation, however hard the pro-pot campaigners try to suggest otherwise. The other key distinction is that alcohol has historically been within the adult culture, and in that sense has more knowingly spread into the youth culture. Illegal drugs have spread through the youth culture with most adults untouched or ignorant.

Thus, although primary prevention work around alcohol would be a lead balloon if it were to suggest lifetime abstinence, it has to make clear that drinking **during adolescence** is not recommended. Studies have shown that if a young person can stay clear of alcohol and tobacco until 20, they are virtually never likely to use illegal drugs. There may be other ways of achieving mature sobriety, but this is an important structural approach which should not be dismissed lightly.

Perhaps the best way of approaching the idea of sobriety (not abstinence) is to break down the idea that alcohol is "different". It is in fact a drug and potentially as damaging as any street drug. Looking then at the reasons why people use drugs and how to counter these reasons (see Chapter 6) one can distil the conclusion that you don't **need** alcohol, and your **want** of some kind of sensory gratification which alcohol gives can be achieved by other activities which don't have the disadvantages of alcohol.

For such an approach to succeed the prevention has to precede onset of alcohol consumption i.e. in the second half of primary school. In the short term in Britain this is unlikely to happen, therefore harm reduction for alcohol becomes appropriate, in terms of consumption limits for adolescents and for primary age children as young as 5. These cannot be the same as the limits suggested by the Health Education Authority for adults (21 units/week for men, 14 for women). There is ample evidence of the greater impact of alcohol on adolescents; taking just one example, alcoholism can occur in adult men after 5-8 years heavy drinking, in women after 3 years, but in adolescents after 2 years down to as little as 6 months in extreme cases. Research just published (quoted in "Young People Now" Issue 32, December 1991, page 11) suggests that pregnant women should cut down to 8 units compared to their normal 14 unit limit (and just before and for a while after conception should be abstinent, to avoid the risks to the child and themselves). It follows that lower consumption levels are relevant for youth, and it is only left then for you to decide whether the figure should be something (say 2 units/week?) or, as per American style, nothing.

## Retrospective

In concluding this overview of professional response/fashions there should be some mention of tertiary prevention i.e. treatment and rehabilitation. Here too there are signs of a shift in approach. At the treatment end there are now new generations of doctors coming through who no longer see the Medical Model of problem drug use as the whole question, let alone the whole answer. They are prepared to take a holistic approach to a user with problems, networking with other agencies such as counselling, psychotherapy, social services - even alternative medicine, to provide a tailored treatment. In the therapeutic communities there are units providing a drug-free drug rehabilitation. It is salutory to observe the processes and goals included in 'typical' rehabilitation; they are in fact almost exactly what one delivers in a prevention programme i.e. the tools to live a drug-free life. The more you think about this the more it makes sense.

Some units, like St Stephen's Mission in Hong Kong or Yeldall Manor in Berkshire employ the power of Christian charismatic revelation and sustained prayer with healing by touch to carry a user through withdrawal. Others like the Core Trust in Northwest London use herbal remedies, acupressure, and other non-drug applications to achieve the same result.

The last word from this area belongs to the users themselves. Experimental users have been known to knock prevention, mainly because it reminds them of where they are. But for users who have gone far enough into use to need counselling or even rehabilitation to recover there is a consistent and unequivocal answer to queries about whether one is right to try and prevent drug/alcohol abuse. Their answer is "You've got it right. Go for it!"

| DATE | SUBSTANCE | ADDICTION /NON-ADDICTION? | MEDICAL MODEL | CRIMINALIZATION | EFFECTS |
|---|---|---|---|---|---|
| 1500 BC | Opium | No records of addiction or problems related to its use. | | | |
| 9C | Opium | Widely used in China and Far East no addiction recognised. | | | |
| 17C | Opium | No addiction problems in West. | Commonly prescribed medical remedy in West. | | Used recreationally in China. |
| 18C | Opium | No addiction problems in West. | Commonly prescribed medical remedy in West. | Prohibited in China - smuggled in from India. | Opium grown in India. Britain sets up smuggling networks to supply China. Huge profits. |
| 19C | Opium & Morphine | 'Recreational' use in West. Addiction now recognised but no stigma & no problems. | Used freely - beginnings of an association between addiction & weakness of character. Addiction accepted as a disease. Drugs freely available. | China now has 3 million addicts. | Opium wars in China. |
| Early 20C | Opiates | Addiction common & recognised but still no problems associated with it. | Addicts regarded as poor victims by physicians. | General public see addicts as lacking in responsibility & Opium use as immoral. | Double standards apparent - press campaign against Opium smoking yet carry adverts for Morphine medicines. |
| 1909 | Opium & Heroin | Physicians repudiate Heroin because of addiction. | | Addicts become 'bad'. | Heroin seen by Press as threat to youth |
| 1913 | Opiates | Addiction | | Trading to China ends. Public opinion changes - addiction now 'evil' & addicts associated with moral harm. | |

**Figure 3.1 (Part 1) Brief History of Opiate Use**

| DATE | SUBSTANCE | ADDICTION /NON-ADDICTION? | MEDICAL MODEL | CRIMINALIZATION | EFFECTS |
|---|---|---|---|---|---|
| 1914 | Opiates | Addiction | | Harrison Act passed in USA. | Control of narcotics & addicts passed to Treasury Dept. who enforce legislation. |
| 1919 - 1923 | Opiates | Addiction | Special Clinics not successful. Public Health Dept. in USA steps out of treatment arena. | Medical approach total failure. Addicts seen as deviants. | |
| 1920's - 1950's | Opiates | Addiction | | Addicts seen as criminals. | More & more government funds allocated to "drugs problems". |
| 1950's - 1960's | Opiates | Addiction | Renewed interest in addiction by physicians in USA. Introduction of special clinics in Britain reinforces the medical model. | Bureau of Narcotics & Dangerous Drugs still unwilling to relinquish control of drugs. | Law enforcement strategies seen to be a failure - public opinion swings back towards the medical model - high hopes of success with Methadone treatment. |
| 1970's | Opiates | Addiction | Methadone treatment not as successful as at first thought. | Black market in Methadone developes. | More Government intervention. Critics refer to Methadone treatment as a means of social control. |
| 1980's | Opiates | Addiction | Addicts seen as patients. | Dealers seen as criminals. | Still a search for a drug to cure drug addiction. |



Figure 3.1 (Part 2) Brief History of Opiate Use

# CHAPTER 3

# THE LEGALISATION MOVEMENT

There have probably been protagonists of more (and less) "liberal" attitudes to drugs for as long as people have used them, and historians proper can effect a better job than this writer in charting the long term evolution of the "War **About** Drugs". Figure 3.1 gives a compressed summary of the history of opiate use. This chapter has the more modest objective of observing the recent activity in so far as it affects the prevention worker. And it **will** affect the worker, for the emergence of effective prevention initiatives is perceived as a threat to the legalisation movement, and, as such must therefore be nobbled by fair means or foul. If you can be sure of one thing, when you commit to prevention work, it is that you will be attacked.

Not every country is treading the libertarian path. A Malaysian delegate at a Far East drugs conference in 1987 dismissed counselling as more suited to the Western "cult of the individual" than to Eastern culture, then went on to list his country's penal responses for all sorts of offences. The death penalty seemed to be ubiquitous, (except perhaps for parking offences?). See Figure 3.2.

In our sector of the globe the responses are indeed more liberal,but by no means consistent, even within a given country. Thus in Europe we have recently had a near-solid affirmation of the UN Single Convention which maintains the illegality of the presently-illegal drugs (including cannabis). But we also have the EMNDP - European Movement for the Normalisation of Drug Policy, the UK branch of which is located in exotic Swindon, and of course we have the Amsterdam coffee shops - hailed by the pro-druggies the world over as a vision of the decriminalised utopian future for us all. Not too many paces away are the decriminalised sex boutiques which attract as many window-shoppers as Harrods at Christmas. The parallels between the two might be worthy of further exploration outside of this publication. Initial thoughts are that prostitution has had a more ambivalent response over the centuries than has cannabis, for which the thumb has been all but consistently down; also, the Amsterdam experiment with formalised prostitution over more than twenty- five years has done nothing to persuade the majority of the world to concur. Amsterdam may be the Mecca for some, but for others, including not a few Netherlanders, the image ranks alongside Bangkok and Las Vegas for its tacky indulgence of hedonism.

Returning to the EMNDP, and leaving aside that Swindon (which also has the highest divorce rate in the country) may, of itself, be a strong reason to do drugs, the key word in their title is Normalisation. In this, EMNDP are in line with their bedmates in America whose very acronym is NORML (National Organisation for Reform of Marijuana Laws).

**COP THIS! MALAYSIAN DRUG PENALTIES**

The Dangerous Drugs Act 1952 prohibited the use, manufacture, sale and importation of all types of narcotics drugs. The penalty for the possession of:

**Heroin, Morphine and Monoacetyl-morphines:**

less than 2 grammes, the fine is not more than MR$20,000.00 and/or not more than 5 years imprisonment

2 grammes or more but not exceeding 5 grammes, the sentence is 2-5 years imprisonment and 3-9 strokes of the rotan

5 grammes or more but less than 15 grammes, a prison term of 5 years to life imprisonment and 10 strokes of the rotan

the death penalty for 15 grammes or more.

**Cocaine:**

less than 5 grammes, a fine not exceeding MR$20,000.00 and/or a prison term of not more than 5 years

5 grammes or more but less than 15 grammes, a prison term of 2-5 years and 3-5 strokes of the rotan

15 grammes or more but less than 40 grammes, the sentence is 5 years to life imprisonment and 10 strokes of the rotan

the death penalty for 40 grammes and above.

**Cannabis and Cannabis Resin:**

less than 20 grammes, a fine not exceeding MR$20,000.00 and/or a prison term not exceeding 5 years

20 grammes or more but less than 50 grammes, 2-5 years imprisonment and 3-9 strokes of the rotan

50 grammes or more but less than 200 grammes, 5 years to life imprisonment and 10 strokes of the rotan

the death penalty for 200 grammes or more.

**Raw Opium and Prepared Opium:**

less than 100 grammes, a fine not exceeding MR$20,000.00 and/or 5 years imprisonment

100 grammes or more but less than 250 grammes, 2-5 years imprisonment and 3-9 strokes of the rotan

250 grammes or more but less than 1,000 grammes, 5 years imprisonment and 10 strokes of the rotan

the death penalty for 1,000 grammes or more.

Source: The Hon Dato Megat Junit bin Megat Ayob, 1987

**Figure 3.2 The Legal Response in the Far East**

Two other examples of this under-stated respectability in titling are the Drug Policy Foundation in Washington DC, and the International Journal of Drug Policy which is based (editorially) on Merseyside. All of these entities support moves towards legalisation of some drugs at least, but they have learnt the strategic value of subtlety. The word Legalisation may turn off 95% of the public but who shall gainsay Normalisation? Humanity, it is argued, is the spur; drug users are too often inhumanely stigmatised and negatively stereotyped, and this can deter them from coming forward for help. Making them feel normal will allow them to function without this burden of disapproval and encourage them to contact agencies.

An example is the (British) Harm Reduction training pack "Taking Drugs Seriously" - a hilarious and doubtless deliberate ambiguity of title - which in the introduction suggests:

> "If attitudes to drug users remain negative, the mythology that surrounds drug use will continue. Drug users are likely to be excluded from the best people who can offer support and help i.e. their own community and peers".

Taking this medicine in two spoonfuls, the corollary of sentence one is that if attitudes to drug users become positive, mythology will disappear ... interview any group of users, young or old and the fatuousness of this will soon come clear. As for sentence two, if drug use is as beneficial and low-risk as the authors imply it can be, why should users need "support and help"? ... the authors have in fact fallen into their own trap of stereotyping users according to a deficit model. This is particularly ironic in the face of much dismissal of prevention approaches as "deficit -model based".

One can see some pros as well as cons in any move to encourage greater contact between drug users and agencies, however this is not the whole agenda. EMNDP in their planning have made the full agenda clear. Quoting from the Mersey Drugs Journal (Vol. 2, No. 6):

> "Two strategies were debated:
>
> (a) Pressurising for regulation of drug production and supply, which might allow others to move out from the middle ground of drug policy.
>
> (b) Pressurising for the less radical objective of decriminalisation of possession of drugs, which might win more initial support.
>
> It was proposed that strategy (b) might be more realistic.
>
> The British Section are also quoted in the article as including in their aims "to encourage a trend towards developing alternative policies which normalise drug taking "

NORML was founded around 1970, principally concentrates on the status of cannabis and does so with the assistance of many articulate and eloquent members. Arnold Trebach, Kevin Zeese, Andrew Weil, Ed Brecher (now deceased), Lester Grinspoon and Norman Zinberg (also now deceased). Another well-known member of the Board is Playboy Chief Hugh Hefner. Abbie Hofmann (also now deceased) does at least use honesty in his book titling i.e. "Steal this Urine Test", unlike the others who cloak their arguments in stylised neo-erudition.

There are some surprises within their teachings, overlooked by many of their disciples who have not read the fine print. Trebach in one of his contributions "Why we are losing the Great Drug War and Radical Proposals that could make America safe Again" - even the title is weighty - argues that NORML is "strongly committed to the concept that growing up should be drug-free ... thus NORML has pushed not pot for youth but reform of the laws through legal means so that adults would be freed of criminal controls". So, let's make pot legal for adults but tell the kids to stay off it until they've grown up. (Just like they do now with tobacco and alcohol) ... Taking this tendentious sleight of hand into account, the lead credit on the book jacket becomes even more outrageous. A "professor of Harvard Medical School", no less, sings Arnold's praises as a man of "sincerity and objectivity" for whom you have no need of "worrying about the author's bias, an achievement in a field characterised by dissension and contradictions". Said professor is Norman Zinberg, and he omits to mention that he is a co-member with Arnold of the board of NORML.

Primary prevention workers and not a few others will of course be angered by Trebach's transparently dishonest rhetoric but the more so should every parent; angry at the insult to their intelligence and the intelligence of anyone else who has the faintest experience of real-life interaction with adolescents. If anything is more calculated to provoke youth into trying something it is to say that we (the adult) can use it but you (the youth) cannot. Even trying to reason your way through such a dialogue would be like trying to walk backwards through a minefield you yourself had laid before inadvertently losing the map. Put another way:

> "There's nothing wrong with an adolescent
> that reasoning with him won't aggravate".

That is of course a sardonic remark but still and all it has the grain of experienced wisdom running through it. It follows therefore that a better strategy is to develop behaviour patterns in adults that do not provoke envy, emulation or otherwise undesirable reaction in youth. If such behaviour can be explained in rational terms it will stand a better chance of beneficially influencing youth, though of course the perversity factor will still be present.

Instinctively grabbing the wrong end of the stick is not solely the prerogative of the young, of course. Anyone seeking to rationalise their use of drugs will shut out any data not matching their current ideology. This is why Arnold Trebach's homily on youth abstention falls on deaf ears. Perhaps more attention-grabbing are the words of conservative libertarian Milton Freidmann. His shock for followers of liberty came when they learned that his commitment to Freedom of the Individual extends to

## THE SPEED LIMIT MODEL

| STRATEGY | CONFERENCE OF MINISTERS LONDON 1990 110 NATIONS | ALASKA (USA) 1983 - 1991 | PRO- DRUG PRESSURE GROUPS | EVERYONE AGREES 'NO' TO THIS |
|---|---|---|---|---|
| | DRUG-FREE | "RECREATIONAL" USE | REGULAR USE | ADDICTION (DEPENDENCY) |
| | 50 | 70 | 90 | 120 |
| | ALL ILLEGAL | DECRIMINALISE | LEGALISE | |
| CONSEQUENCES: | | | | |
| HEALTH: (PHYS) | GOOD | SMALL DAMAGE | HIGHEST COST TO NATION | A FEW PEOPLE COST A LOT EACH |
| (MIND) | GOOD | SMALL DAMAGE | LARGE NUMBERS DAMAGED | SMALL NUMBERS VERY DAMAGED |
| (EMOTION & SPIRIT) | GOOD | RISKY | UNHEALTHY | VERY BAD |
| SOCIAL COST | ZERO | SIGNIFICANT | HIGHEST COST | A FEW PEOPLE COST A LOT EACH |
| COMMUNITY BENEFIT | PLUS | MINUS | HIGHEST COST | LESS COST, BUT STILL LARGE |
| CRIME | LESS | MORE | MUCH MORE | LARGE PER PERSON |

**Any speed limit will be exceeded by some. Limit at 50 will mean some do 70, limit at 70 means some do 90. Highest cost to nation is 90, therefore discourage all from reaching this. Alaska decriminalisation of cannabis brought massive increases in use of this and all other drugs, also in problem users (with health/social/societal costs) and crime overall increased. Alaska therefore reverted to a 50 speed limit.**



**Figure 3.3 The Effect of Varying Controls**

problem drug users. You're on your own in deciding to use, but you're also on your own if you become a casualty, so don't look to society to put right what you individually induced. As Michael Caine would say "Not a lot of people know that". And when a lot of people came to know it via a radio phone-in programme favoured by practitioners of the weed, it unleashed many shocked calls. Anti-drug attorney Bob Peterson, invited to come on air to make a fool of himself, had instead delivered a cruise missile to mission control.

Many working professionally or parentally (or both) with young people recognise the need for and developmental value of Boundary-Setting; another anathema for the libertarian. Young people will always push against and sometimes exceed any boundaries that are set; if there are no boundaries the youth themselves can be at a loss. If one considers a 'speed limit' model as shown in Figure 3.3, there are four suggested speeds; Drug-Free, Occasional Use, Regular Use and Dependent Use. The prevention worker will set the limit at Drug-Free, knowing that some will exceed to Occasional. If one takes a sanguine view towards Occasional Use then many more will speed up to Regular Use. From data on alcohol-related consequences it is known that the Regular user costs the country overall far more than the Dependents (of whom there are much fewer).

## Capitol Idea

The innocuously-named Drug Policy Foundation in Washington DC must have one of the best images of all the drug reform lobbies. They hold meetings in no less a venue than the White House! The Old Executive Office, next to the White House proper (so called when it had to be painted all over to cover the soot after the British burnt it in 1812), is used as a Drug Policy Foundation rendevous, and members are invited to meet influential government officials and even be put in touch with those who can assist them to become influential government officials themselves. Amongst their fans is millionaire commodities trader Richard J Dennis, who has bankrolled them for 2 million dollars over five years. Try to imagine a British minority interest pressure group having a more or less permanent presence in the Palace of Westminster, able to buttonhole MPs in the corridors, and you have some idea of what is happening in Washington.

The Drug Policy Foundation, like its partners, outwardly promotes itself as an objective seeker of the truth, content to press for no more than sanity in policies towards drug users. A cursory examination of its membership and of the proceedings of its seminars make the real situation clear enough. Their Reformer's Catalogue (1989-90), editors Arnold Trebach (again) and Kevin Zeese runs to 451 pages and claims to contain latest ideas from "some" of the leading thinkers in the field of drug policy. Surpisingly enough this random selection of leading thinkers all concur that Drug War is bad, what we need is Drug Peace. This even extends in some cases to the use (or abuse) of mathematical models to support contentious propositions. One mathematician (Caulkins) takes 25 pages full of lengthy complex equations (see Figure 3.4 for a sample) to conclude that his model, to challenge zero tolerance policy as a means of minimising use, is

> "not suitable for quantitatively computing the optimal punishment policy ... the model makes many assumptions ... it also ignores important issues ... most significantly though, the policies prescribed are functions of the user's utility parameters. These parameters cannot be measured ...".

With the author in such a defeatist frame of mind, critics are scarcely necessary. Both this paper and the succeeding mathematical study (examining the psychology of the War on Drugs) by Rosing, have been examined by a British mathematician not connected with drug work in any way. His critique, equally full of equations, may be boiled down to scepticism over the one conclusion Caulkins doesn't himself destroy i.e. that zero tolerance may not minimise consumption, and a scathing dismissal of Rosing as "simply playing with symbols, the sociological significance of which he is totally ignorant". At a more prosaic level, Caulkins could be said to be arguing that zero tolerance as he understands it, with the same punishment however much you use, is likely to provoke increased use ... ("might as well be hung for a sheep as a lamb") etc. This is Boy's Book of Sociology stuff; even though one can equally argue that tough across-the-board penalties will discourage some from using, neither of these simplistic scenarios deserves to be used as a sole basis for policy.

The Drug Policy Foundation's aim of placing staff in key positions is no mere pipedream, appropriate though that metaphor may be. During

utility, the new optimal solution's utility must be at least as great. In symbols,

$$z(\bar{f}, \tilde{q}; \tfrac{c_a}{Q}q) \geq z(F, Q; \tfrac{c_a}{Q}q) = z(F, Q; c_a(q) = c_a).$$

Actually the inequality is strict because

$$z(\bar{f}, \tilde{q}; \tfrac{c_a}{Q}q) - z(F, Q; c_a(q) = c_a)$$

$$= \frac{\alpha\left(\frac{\alpha}{2} - \sqrt{h(c_s + p\,c_a)}\right)}{c_p\left(c_pQ + p\,c_a\right)}\left(\sqrt{\frac{c_s + p\,c_a}{2}} - \sqrt{\frac{c_s}{2}}\right)^2 > 0.$$

Also, the user will buy more frequently since

$$\bar{f} - F = \frac{\frac{\alpha}{2} - \sqrt{h(c_s + p\,c_a)}}{2\,c_p\left(c_pQ + p\,c_a\right)}\left[\alpha\left(\sqrt{\frac{c_s + p\,c_a}{c_s}} - 1\right) + \sqrt{\frac{h}{c_s + p\,c_a}}\,2\,p\,c_a\right] > 0.$$

**Figure 3.4 Mathematics Screws You Up**

Jimmy Carter's presidency there was a flirtation with the so-called "British System" of maintenance-prescribing for dependents; even talk of legalising heroin for medical uses and decriminalising possession of small quantities of cannabis for "recreational" use. Just why these radical reforms came so close to approval was explained when President Carter's Adviser on substance abuse matters, Dr Peter Bourne, disclosed that he was a board member of NORML.

Bourne and NORML Director, Keith Stroup, miscalculated badly when at the NORML Christmas Party in 1977 they openly ingested cocaine in front of news reporters. Though this was kept under wraps for several months, when Bourne was later implicated in illegal prescribing of methaqualone to a friend, the whole story broke, and within a year both Bourne and Stroup were out of their jobs.

It is not known whether the President's Adviser came through the Drug Policy Foundation's old boy network, but the system is openly promoted. In its 1989 International Conference, The Drug Policy Foundation trumpetted the launch of its "first Professional Employment Exchange to publicise opportunities in academia, research, law, treatment, criminal justice and advocacy, and to connect job hunters discreetly with possible openings".

## Comic Cuts

If the Drug Policy Foundation epitomises the establishment approach to liberalism, the opposite end of the spectrum surely belongs to High Times magazine. Launched in 1974, in its heady (?) days it sold more than a million copies in a month. The US population is 260 million, so market penetration was not massive. However, it was significant and would have been augmented by more than one person reading each copy.

When millionaire High Times founder Tom Forcade committed suicide in 1978 the magazine began to lose its drive. Sales slumped to 250,000 by the mid 80s and have stayed little above that figure ever since. From a peak staff level of 100 which included back-up staff to cover for anyone too stoned to work, establishment has shrunk to the present staff of 8. They work to an annual budget of perhaps 1.5 million dollars, and drug taking in the office is no longer tolerated; promoting drug use is serious business. Taking drugs seriously, once more.

**SECRET OPERATIONS**

☐ **THE CONSTRUCTION AND OPERATION OF CLANDESTINE DRUG LABORATORIES,** ***by Jack B. Nimble,*** reveals how to select a location for a clandestine drug laboratory, how to cover your tracks, safety precautions, and when and how to shut down your operation to keep out of the slammer. ***This book is sold for informational purposes only. 1986, 5½ x 8½, 60 pp, illustrated, soft cover.*** **$13.00 postpaid.**

High Times is a 100 page monthly with full-colour on many pages. As such it is a step or two above the kind of 'underground' journals we see in Britain. Cartoon characters such as Ed Hassle invite the reader to fund the legalisation fight. Adverts abound for cannabis seeds, cultivation hardware, and text books/systems. A few ads tackle even more 'specialised' activities; for example, the display shown here.

A reader's letter in High Times, April 1989, gives an interesting insight into their editorial policy (or maybe strategy would be closer) and ties in closely with Arnold Trebach's dictum against drug use by youth, quoted earlier in this chapter. A young Floridian converted from anti-pot to pro-pot after reading High Times has written in to relate how he now campaigns for legalising cannabis. The editor replies:

> "Although cannabis is one of the safest drugs known to man - safer than alcohol, nicotine, caffeine or aspirin - it must be treated with respect. High Times does not encourage the use of cannabis by high school students. Your letter was very heartwarming to us, but minors should concentrate on improving their minds first. Psychedelic mind expansion is best left until after graduation".

Maybe this is tongue-in-cheek rhetoric. Maybe the fact that the DEA are amongst the regular purchasers of the magazine prompted this grab for brownie points. For sure, no High-School reader would fail to pick up the pro-pot remarks and the implicit message that "psychedelic mind expansion" is something to which one may aspire when grown up. And the "Wet Paint - Don't Touch" syndrome would come into play once more, as it so often does with youth.

Britain has no such wacky pro-drug publications yet. Our cartoon publications are generally related to harm reduction. The best- known example is the "Smack in the Eye" comic published by Lifeline, Manchester. A Scottish equivalent emerged later. Both publications can legitimately claim to be mainly addressing people who have already elected to use, and the assumption is made that for users a prevention message is obsolete. This is arguable; for some this could be a very impactful message if handled right, coming somewhere within a harm reduction comic; especially as not every reader will be a user.

Of some concern too is the use of rough characters and even rougher language. The authors feel the youth relate to this better. It would be interesting to see a sociologically valid evaluation of this (stigmatising and stereotyping) editorial policy; whether it is beneficial or whether it is self-indulgent and misguided. If drug use is as "normal" as some claim, perhaps the cartoon characters should reflect this normalcy in their characters.

Back in the establishment area of campaigning, British readers looking for "liberalist" succour can turn to the International Journal on Drug Policy. Born out of the Merseyside Drug Journal, the International comes in a striking jet-black wrap-around cover, and features mostly sober and discursive articles as to why most of Britain has got it wrong in preventing drugs. It is a quality production with an international cast, the members of which make for interesting reading. The "Contributing

Editors" include Andrew Weil, Ethan Nadelmann, Arnold Trebach (and until their demise Norman Zinberg and Ed Brecher) - all the old NORML/DPF groupies. British-based contributors include many of the anti-prevention lobby, making it clear that until now at least this publication is a crusader rather than a provider of balanced observation. British writers include Alan Matthews, Pat O'Hare, Betsy Ettore, Cindy Fazey, Russell Newcombe, Allan Parry, and Andrew Tyler. Pat O'Hare was a guest speaker at DPF's conference in Maryland in October 1988 when his paper entitled "Drug Education - a Basis for Reform" was presented. The paper argues for a review of educational systems, and does so in a restrained and sober manner. The tape transcript of the session gives a very different picture. Listeners are informed that "England has absolutely nothing to learn from America," that "this 12-step (AA) rubbish is cr*p". ("What are the 12 steps?" asks the audience. "I dunno" he replies), and that delegates should earnestly consider "If kids can't have fun with drugs when they're kids, when can they have fun with them?". The silence that followed this little gem, pierced only by the odd embarrassed giggle, was especially illuminating given the constitution of the audience. (i.e. when it comes to radicalism we Brits can show the former colonies a thing or two).

There are at last some signs of the International Journal seeking other points of view. This may be partly linked to a change of publisher brought about by their recent financial problems, or may be a strategic shift; change the window dressing but keep the main bill of goods the same. (It is hard not to be drawn into cynicism in this environment). Other Journal contributors include Carol Tongue MEP, who was one of only five European signatories to a minority paper in 1986 dissenting with Europe's prevention approach to drug policy. The dissenters accused the Committee Rapporteur, Sir Jack Stewart- Clark, of a "tendentious approach" (adverb; "with an underlying purpose, intended to further a cause"). One might well observe on pot (no pun intended) calling kettle black. Dr Nicholas Dorn is published in the journal in addition to his frequent articles in Druglink, the magazine of the Institute for the Study of Drug Dependence, for which he is the Research Director. Nick gets tough with primary prevention more often than not, and advocates harm reduction as the alternative. If evaluations of prevention look good they are suspected of infection from the "halo effect" i.e. the project is new so everyone wants to believe in it and say nice things about it. However, if evaluations are bad they vindicate his hypothesis, viz prevention is impossible. All this in spite of his feeling compelled to remark in a recent prevention overview that

> "in spite of the resources brought to bear in evaluations, we are simply not in a position to make a fully informed judgement on prevention."

Does all this smack of the tendentious? Or is it just that Harm Reduction is dazzling him with its "halo effect?". Time will tell.

The list of pushers for hedonism is long. Two more, which should be enough for now, are IAPL and ICAR. IAPL, the International Anti-

Prohibitionist League founded in 1989 is conveniently located in Brussels as 1992 heralds a more Eurocentric age. The IAPL reroasts the old chestnuts about prohibition having failed to prevent drug growth, having encouraged criminal networks who endanger the good citizen and destabilise the good government ... Prohibition brings harassment for the casual user and stigma for heavier users, costs a fortune and discredits the legal system which is forced to enact silly laws. Best of all, "prohibition has become a major obstacle to effective drug education". How so? "Attributing power to drugs diminishes personal responsibility". This author would welcome an intelligible explanation of what the above two statements mean, and how they hang together.

ICAR, the International Cannabis Alliance for Reform was born in 1978 out of an encounter recalling the era of the good ship Mayflower. Rev. William Deane, Pennsylvania Co-ordinator for NORML got together with Tom Malyon of England. Malyon co-authored, with Betsy Ettore and others, the book "Big Deal - the Politics of the Illicit Drugs Business". Published in Britain in 1985 this is a good read, but subtly argues for legalisation and harm reduction. Recognising that an internationalist front would be needed to challenge the 1961 United National Single Convention on Narcotic Drugs (signed by over 100 countries), Deane and Malyon sought out reformers in Canada, Italy, Holland, Denmark and Australia. By the end of the year ICAR was officially inaugurated. ICAR sought recognition by the UN during the early 80s as an NGO (non-governmental organisation) dealing with human rights. This would allow them to attend and address UN functions. Although this was refused they were awarded observer status which gave them access to most UN meetings. Given that most institutions find that much of their business is furthered not in the meetings, but in the coffee breaks, lunches, and corridors, this gift of proximity will undoubtedly have been exploited to the full.

## Drawing the Threads Together

From this chapter so far it can be seen that there is a richly variegated species of antagonists to prevention. The full extent is difficult to measure, partly because those who are pro-drug often keep their heads down, and partly because this is a volatile area of social politics; by the time this book is published there may well be significant changes in the organisations described.

Nevertheless, it is valuable for a prevention worker to become informed and keep abreast of this area of his/her work, no less than in all other areas. There may well be questions put to a prevention worker by a lay audience, or by such as teachers, based on arguments they have heard advanced on TV/radio etc. When Judge Pickles first entered the media arena in 1991 on the subject of drug legalisation it generated enough interest to provoke many questions to prevention workers at the time. For those able to answer the Judge's assertions with solid facts, illustrating that the information he worked from came from biased sources, this was a good opportunity to strengthen the case for prevention.

Public debate does not however seem to suit the palate of the typical prevention worker. Because he/she is essentially concerned with promoting the positives in life, responding to aggressive initiatives by critics is something to be skated around. A further factor militating against esprit de corps is that the body of evaluation supporting prevention work is slim. There are sound reasons for this (see Chapter 1) but when one is under fire, reasons are poor protection. Prevention has almost never been funded with evaluation adequately resourced, and until it is so funded evaluation will remain an Achilles Heel.

## Common Reasons for and Against Legalisation

Many "upper school" training packs contain exercises around propositions to legalise one or more drugs. Others take the more radical starting hypothesis that a new substance has been found or invented with "the following effects" (insert cannabis information, for example). In both cases discussion groups will pool arguments for and against, then return to debate the proposition. It may prove more conducive to take all the pro-drug arguments first, or one may decide to ask for alternate assertions from each side, to keep the interest alive. Certainly one will find a very full 'blackboard' in half an hour or less, and young people are just as good as adults at coming up with the assertions. A typical collection of assertions is given in Figure 3.5.

It is some measure of the penetration by permissivists that the arguments in favour of legalisation come in thick and fast, compared to arguments against. The other reason for this of course is the ready adoption of pro-drug (and scepticism of no-drug) assertions by many (but not all) in the media. Whether it is the "Good News is No News" syndrome or whether media members as a species incline more towards drugs, the bottom line is that prevention workers find it extremely difficult to get space in the media; this has been found in Europe and America as well as Britain.

There are of course still more assertions that can be made on both sides, and many of the above points could generate an evening's discussion on their own! There is a fine irony in suggesting that the marketing of drugs should be taken out of the hands of criminals and put into the hands of those responsible people, the tobacco and alcohol manufacturers - well worth an hour's debate.

Another gem is the idea that you tax the newly legalised drugs heavily then spend the tax money on persuading young people not to use drugs. This masterpiece of logic came from the pages of one of Britain's 'quality' newspapers, though others have voiced it too.

This assertion appears amongst the "Pros" and "Cons" but there are many more that can be developed. Use Figure 3.5 therefore as a guide rather than a specification.

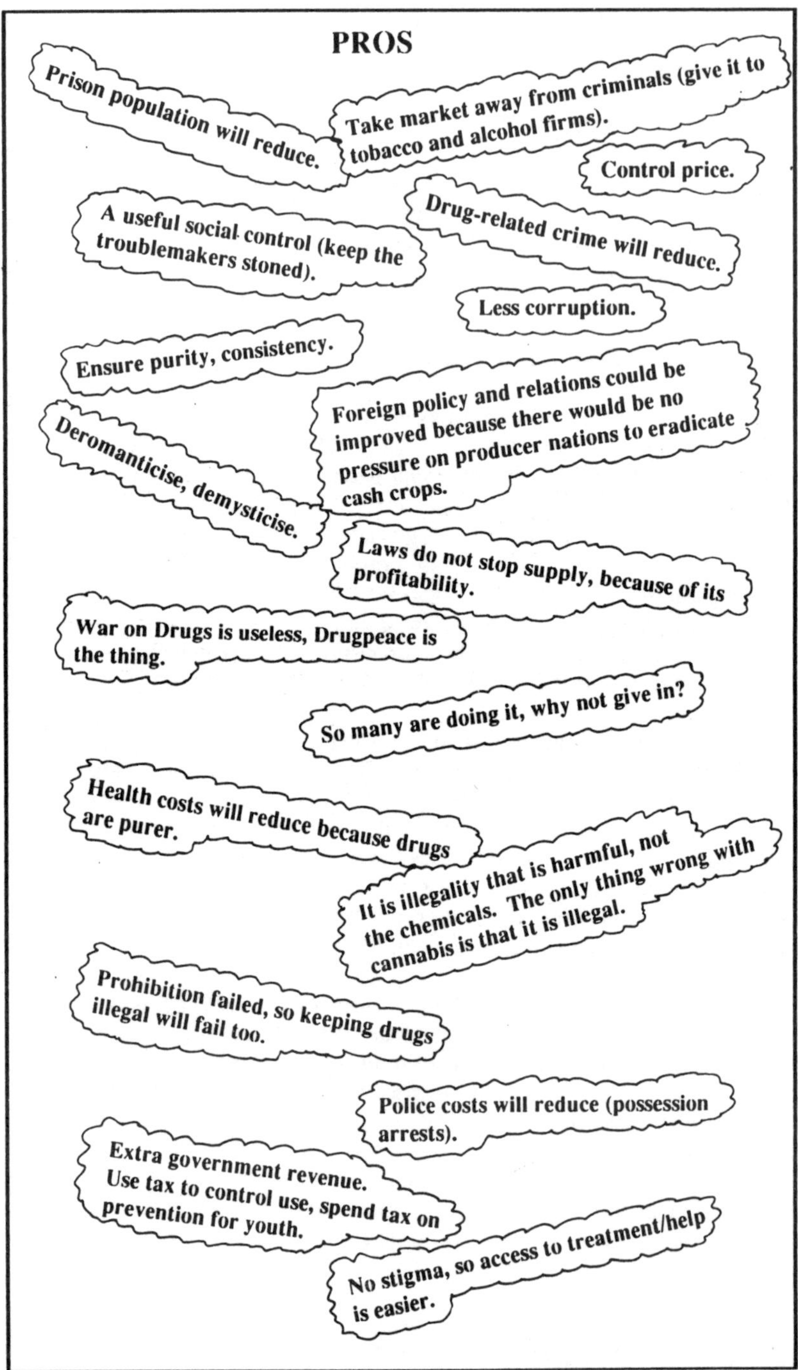


**Figure 3.5 (Part 1) Arguments around Legalisation; Those For**

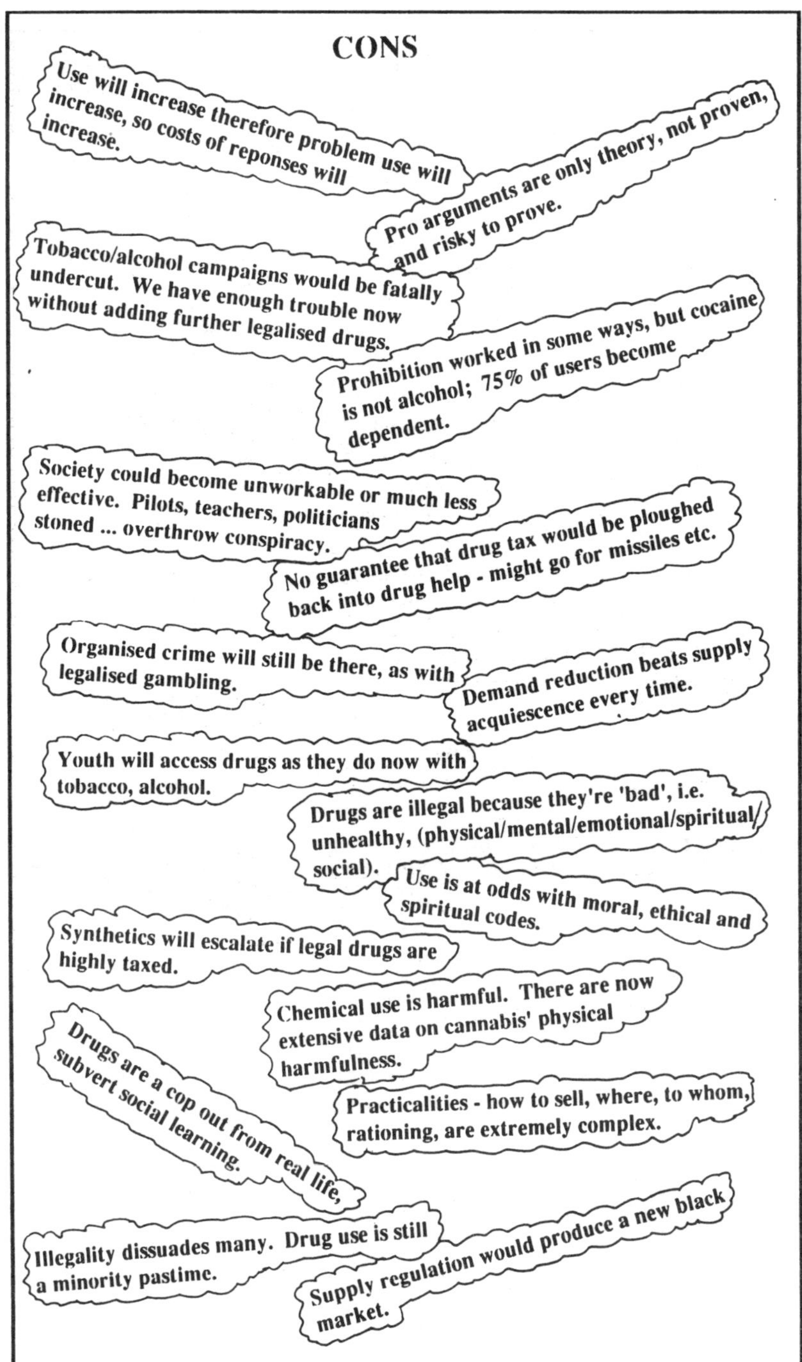

CONS
Use will increase therefore problem use will increase, so costs of reponses will increase.
Pro arguments are only theory, not proven, and risky to prove.
Tobacco/alcohol campaigns would be fatally undercut. We have enough trouble now without adding further legalised drugs.
Prohibition worked in some ways, but cocaine is not alcohol; 75% of users become dependent.
Society could become unworkable or much less effective. Pilots, teachers, politicians stoned ... overthrow conspiracy.
No guarantee that drug tax would be ploughed back into drug help - might go for missiles etc.
Organised crime will still be there, as with legalised gambling.
Demand reduction beats supply acquiescence every time.
Youth will access drugs as they do now with tobacco, alcohol.
Drugs are illegal because they're 'bad', i.e. unhealthy, (physical/mental/emotional/spiritual/social).
Use is at odds with moral, ethical and spiritual codes.
Synthetics will escalate if legal drugs are highly taxed.
Chemical use is harmful. There are now extensive data on cannabis' physical harmfulness.
Drugs are a cop out from real life, subvert social learning.
Practicalities - how to sell, where, to whom, rationing, are extremely complex.
Illegality dissuades many. Drug use is still a minority pastime.
Supply regulation would produce a new black market.


**Figure 3.5 (Part 2) Arguments around Legalisation; Those Against**

The Social Control Model (keep troublemakers drugged) versus the Social Revolution Model (drugs make trouble) is also another good topic for debate. In case you should want to dismiss the latter as paranoid hyperbole, consider the following quotation:

> "By making readily available drugs of various kinds; by giving a teenager alcohol; by praising his wildness; by strangling him with sex literature and advertising to him or her ... the psychopolitical preparation can create the necessary attitude of chaos, idleness and worthlessness into which can then be cast the solution that will give the teenager complete freedom everywhere. If we can effectively kill the national pride and patriotism of just one generation, we will have won that country. Therefore, there must be continued propoganda to undermine the loyalty of citizens in general and teenagers in particular".

The author was Josef Stalin. Doubtless the former USSR countries are currently more pre-occupied with internal matters than with external ambitions, but to view the above passage purely in terms of one country or one political ideology is to miss the point.

## Alaska - The Experiment that Failed

In 1972 two young lawyers, Wagstaff and Raven, were smoking grass and bemoaning the illegality of their pleasure. They agreed that the right case with a good client could overturn state law. The next event in this chain was for Raven to be arrested in Alaska in possession of joints. He protested his case on the grounds of violation of his private rights. Legal and financial help was provided by NORML. They lost their case but appealed to the Alaskan Supreme Court who in 1975 ruled five-to-one in favour of Raven, judging that there was no scientific evidence of harm from cannabis and certainly nothing that would justify invasion of privacy. This was subsequently extended to include cultivation as well as possession.

Attempts to recriminalise only resulted in the courts defining "a small amount for personal use" as four ounces - enough for around 300 joints, and a quantity many local-level dealers would regard as a good stock.

The arguments advanced by Raven and his entourage make interesting reading, striking many chords with the tabulation in Figure 3.5. The main arguments were:

(1) Decriminalising cannabis will not increase use; it is so easily available that everyone who wants it now can get it.

(2) Nor will it increase problem use. Those who are heavily enough into it to become problem users are already using.

(3) Nor will it increase the use of other drugs; "as we all know

the Gateway Theory (one drug leads to another) is discredited".

(4) Crime will go down because the vast number of possession charges will disappear, and cannabis is a peacemaker drug.

Mainly because of item (4) the police supported decriminalisation. By the beginning of 1990 monitoring of the situation showed:

(1) Major increase in use, up to twice the national average.
(2) Major increase in problem use, up to twice the national average. Heavy increase in health/social costs.
(3) Use of all other drugs increased.
(4) Crime overall went up.

On reviewing this signal failure of the decriminalisation experiment the law was rescinded, with the full support of the police who were amongst many to have changed their minds in the face of this incontrovertible evidence.

At the end of his 1991 "Byline" programme on the subject of drug legalisation, Judge Pickles said "... Of course, if use were to increase I would have to think again ...". When presented with the above evidence on his subsequent LBC Talkback radio programme the pursuit of liberty was in full swing and there was no sign of thinking again ...

**"And liberty plucks justice by the nose ..."**
(Shakespeare's Measure for Measure).

## Summarising

There are several organisations well versed in pressure group politics. They understand how to make a big noise with small numbers. They know how the lobby system works and how the media circus works. The product they are selling - a freer approach to drug use, is arguably more newsworthy than drug-free life (i.e. free of drugs of abuse). Governments and courts are no less prone to off-centre judgements, when having a bad day, than any other body.

Take heart, however. The arguments in favour of drug-free life are strong and numerous. Health must be measured in more than the narrow terms (physical deterioration with time) chosen by the drug protagonists. One must recognise the validity of the Ancient Greeks' definition of health (physical, mental, emotional, spiritual, social, environmental; refer to Chapter 6 "Health - what is it?") and see how a life involving drugs of abuse falls far short of this. Distil it even further, and talk of liberating a person's potential by keeping them drug free. In this sense **the prevention worker is the true liberal**, not the pro-drug campaigner; all the latter produces is people hobbled at the ankles by drug use - yes, they are experiencing a new sensation, but is it a sensation that has as great a potential for lasting pleasure, fulfilment and achievement that the unhobbled person can obtain?

## CHAPTER 4

# LEARNING FROM THE WORLD

America has a reputation as the place where your hairdresser tells you their life problems instead of listening to yours. This urge for self disclosure has great advantages for foreign students of prevention, for the descriptions of projects and programmes have an invaluable degree of candour. Given that they embarked on serious prevention efforts some twelve years ahead of Britain their stories are well worth hearing, and filtering out any dogma or sales talk is usually easy because of the openness of the presenters. Above all else, Americans seem anxious to have you avoid making the same mistakes they did.

Thus, when a Ministerial group visited America in the mid 80s they were urged to avoid crusades against just one drug - kids then assume the untargetted drugs are OK. (In fact, British Drug Education Co-ordinators at the same time pleaded similarly with the Ministers.) Despite this the Government pressed ahead with their Heroin Screws You Up campaign. The chickens came home to roost as predicted, and kids at large were encountered saying "I wouldn't do smack, terrible stuff like the telly says, but a bit of whizz or blow or acid, if that was well dodgy they'd say so, ennit?".

Openness has its risk, of course. If you open your arms it's easier for someone to smack you in the mouth. The results of a brief foray into America in 1988 by writers for the Mersey Drug Journal demonstrated that. The cover of the subsequent issue of the Journal depicted a GI peering through the undergrowth, with the caption "Drug War - the Americans Go Over the Top". Articles inside superficially dismissed initiatives such as Just Say No clubs, and gave the impression that officials in NIDA (the National Institute on Drug Abuse; Washington DC) were only saluting the prevention flag under duress; secretly "some people" (unnamed) "admitted" what the Journal wanted to hear i.e. prevention "doesn't work".

It would be naive to deny that many Americans run on fuel with the additive of Emotional Commitment, and sometimes the resultant power surge can take them off the road. Surely the answer for the objective foreign student is to keep the emotional component in perspective, take the benefit of its presence in moderation and in relation to one's own culture, but don't ditch it altogether.

America has to be one of the main places to start looking for source initiatives and model experiences in prevention. Other nations have excellent projects too, as this chapter endeavours to show, but for quality and variety the United States is indeed a rich seam to work.

Without doubt the first port of call for prevention workers should be Atlanta, Georgia. Atlanta has many claims to fame - "Gone With the Wind", Coca Cola, CNN (Cable News Network), CDC (Center for Disease

Control, pioneer in AIDS research), Martin Luther King, the Jimmy Carter Center specialising in International Conflict Resolution, Olympics 96, and the "Air Force" slam dunkers of the Atlanta Hawks NBA basketball team. Another sometime sports star with the Atlanta Falcons, NFL Gridiron football team is Mick Luckhurst, and this links conveniently back to the subject of this chapter. Mick is an Englishman and is now presenter of "Red 42" and "American Football" on Britain's Channel 4. He was a kicker for the Falcons, and like many other sports figures he contributed to America's drug prevention efforts by public appearances in a joint sports/DEA programme called "TeamUp". When this author met him he was appearing in Atlanta at the annual conference of the other organisation for which the city can be justly proud - PRIDE, the Parents Resource Institute for Drug Education.

## PRIDE

In 1977 Dr Thomas Gleaton, a Professor, first of Physiology and then of Education at Georgia State University received a visit from another academic, Mrs Marsha Manatt Schuchard. But Marsha was in no mood for academic dialogue. Appalled and concerned by the drug problem facing the country, and speaking as a parent herself, she had been galvanised into action by finding a pot party in progress at her own home. She very assertively pressed the argument that the response to date on drug abuse i.e. information-giving and education (largely didactic) was way off centre. What was needed was a grass roots parents movement which also involved the youth themselves. Buddy was momentarily taken aback, but as a teacher he knew his streetwise students were more knowledgeable about drugs than he was; as a parent of young children himself he could readily connect with Marsha's arguments, and he could hardly fail to be enthused by the possibilities. That same year they launched their first PRIDE Conference. 120 came. Small, but enough...

In 1990 in Orlando, Florida, PRIDE delegates stood outside the convention centre and watched the space shuttle Discovery carry the Hubble telescope safely into space. By the time everyone had entered the centre there were almost 9,000 parents, youth and interested professionals filling the halls and corridors. During the week-long conference there were separate "tracks" run for adults, college age, school age, businessmen, armed services, academics and more, allowing each to thread their way through more than 200 workshops, presentations, rallies, plenary sessions, filmshows, plus more than 100 exhibition stands. Speakers ranged from housewives in the Cayman Islands to Presidents of Nations. George Bush sent his Adviser on Drugs, Bill Bennett, and also sent a personal video message to PRIDE. More than 80 nations were represented in the International Conference which ran within the main schedule.

The Gulf War put a damper on both home and international attendance in 1991 but even so 7,000 turned up to PRIDE XIV in Nashville Tennessee. By the time this book is printed PRIDE XV will have taken place in Houston, Texas, with PRIDE XVI (1993) scheduled for Salt Lake City, Utah.

Over the fourteen years since those two concerned Atlantan parents started PRIDE it has grown to a full time staff of over 60 and a membership of thousands spread across more than half the States of America and internationally. PRIDE organisations exist in Canada, Australia, New Zealand, Egypt, Belize, Cayman Islands, Panama and several more. Links with prevention organisations on all continents, not least Europe, are maintained.

PRIDE are much more than organisers of inspirational conferences. Their year-long schedule involves the development and application of youth and parent programmes and the monitoring of these programmes in action. At several age levels PRIDE run a school- based confidential questionnaire which has been validated by countless repetitions and assessments. Literally millions of young people all over America have completed this questionnaire; for example in one month alone in 1990 over 400,000 youth in Georgia gave their answers. The completed forms are processed by computer to give prevalence levels of each substance, split by age; repetition over a period gives a measure of the effectiveness of any prevention effort.

The PRIDE Survey is the baby of Dr Ronald Adams, Professor of Education at Western Kentucky University. His location may explain why one of PRIDE's most detailed prevention evaluations, a longitudinal study started in 1987 and still going strong, is based in Bowling Green Community, a small settlement in Western Kentucky. With the advantage of proximity Dr Adams has been able to rigourously monitor the situation as Bowling Green initiated and sustained a community prevention programme involving all sectors - education, business, social agencies, sports, religion and so on. Across the five years of records published so far there has been a continuous fall in use of all substances by almost all age groups, the only fluctuation being with younger age groups having small percentage levels of use, where the statistical significance of any variation is probably dubious.

The Bowling Green study is undoubtedly very valuable because of its academic rigour and longevity. The pro-drug lobby would be hard pressed to deny that real prevention achievements are being made in the face of national trends which until recently were almost all upward. The resourcefulness of critics is however equal to that of protagonists of any project. Therefore, protagonists would look at Figure 4.1, see reduction in cannabis use by 12th graders (age 16-17) from 45% to 30% and shout "Success". Critics would see 30% are still using after five years prevention effort and shout "Failure". What you see depends on where you stand.

The central conclusion is nevertheless inescapable, that prevention can be seen to be working.

PRIDE have a number of activities which are headquarters-based, such as publications, videos, reference materials, a help line, consultancy and training, and international affairs. The great majority of time is spent on encouraging and assisting work by the grassroots. In this context, and from among many other resources, two particular programmes deserve special mention.

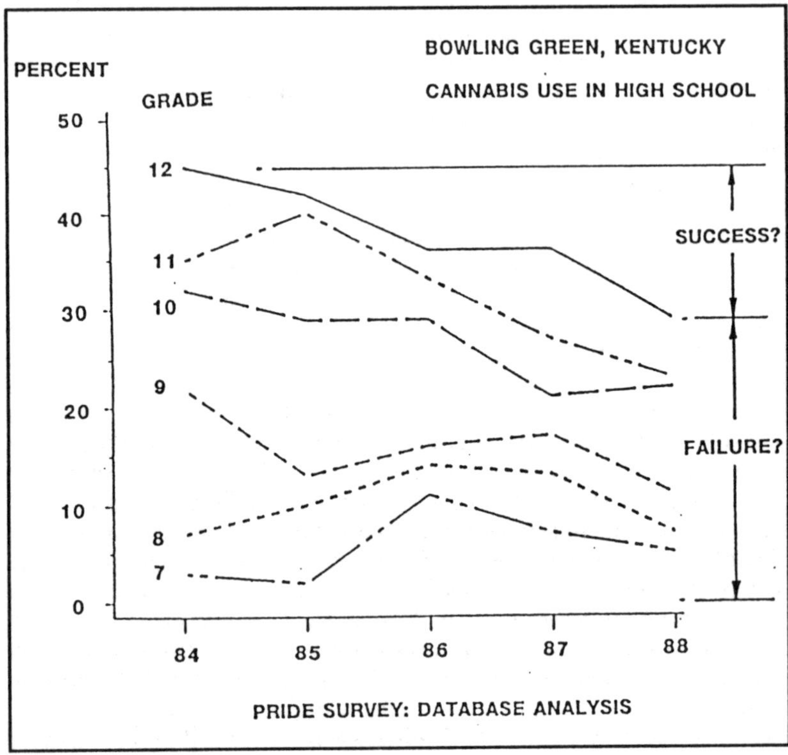


**Figure 4.1 Bowling Green Shows the Way**

## PRIDE Youth Programme

Whilst devoting much energy to such as lifeskill development, drug/alcohol awareness, risky behaviour and harm reduction, the PRIDE youth workers concentrate on encouraging and celebrating a drug-free life, where youth are part of the solution. Youth teams in a large number of states negotiate a schedule of visits to schools and colleges. In each establishment they spend a full day with a large group of students released from their classes.

As the day develops the knowledge/attitudes/behaviour transfer is progressed at the pace of the students, much of it in the form of games, role-plays and skits. The target in all this is a show to be presented to parents and others in the evening. The PRIDE youth workers themselves are polished performers and give a lift to the whole production but the real stars are the members of the school themselves. With expert training by the youth workers the students present skits they have formulated during the day, sing or dance to backing tracks furnished by PRIDE, and share the compering.

What do the students gain from this experience? Education yes, pleasure from drug-free activities yes, self-fulfilment yes, and above all they gain exposure to the possibility that being drug-free can be fulfilling and fun. This shared experience, which is likely to include current users in the school with (some) ex-users in the PRIDE team, often encourages students to set up PRIDE groups in their own schools. Even a group with just one or two students is a bridgehead for future prevention work, and the PRIDE resources are on call.

From within the state teams, a National Performance Team is drawn, giving excellent presentations at major events across the nation. All these young performers are amateur, but only in name.

## Parent-to-Parent

The keystone of prevention work is seen by PRIDE to be The Parent. In the period 1959-1979 the percentage of teenagers who had tried an illegal drug rocketed from 1% to 60%. In the face of this many "experts" and policymakers argued that drug use had become a "socially acceptable" form of behaviour and that America should therefore secede from the UN Single Convention by which 157 nations agree to maintain the illegal status of certain drugs. That this did not happen can be largely credited to sustained pressure by the parent movement, who had not been consulted by either the "experts" or the policymakers as to what constituted socially unacceptable behaviour. (This may strike one or two chords this side of the Atlantic.)

PRIDE's original (1977) Philosophy, which still holds today, is that the strongest prevention stems from the paternal instinct to protect the young (followed by the instinct of the young to protect each other). Figure 4.2 exemplifies this. However, at a time when parents and families are becoming increasingly isolated and fragmented because of changes in social conditions, economic pressures, and community values, parents need all the help they can get; help with maintaining standards in the nurturing and guidance of their children and influence on the immediate environment which affects the growth and development of their children. This help must come from "people who respect parents, who sympathise with their problems, who have faith in their concern for their children, and who believe in their rights to affirm behavioural and ethical standard within their families".

This last extract from the Philosophy is a salutory jolt for many of us who tend to marginalise parents - in one English District Drugs Strategy running to some 4000 words parents were only mentioned once, and then with the qualifying epithet "over-reacting". Parents may indeed sometimes, initially, over-react but soon level down; others will react, quite appropriately; others under-react through fear; and others - the real gems - will be pro-active, innate prevention workers. This is why PRIDE's

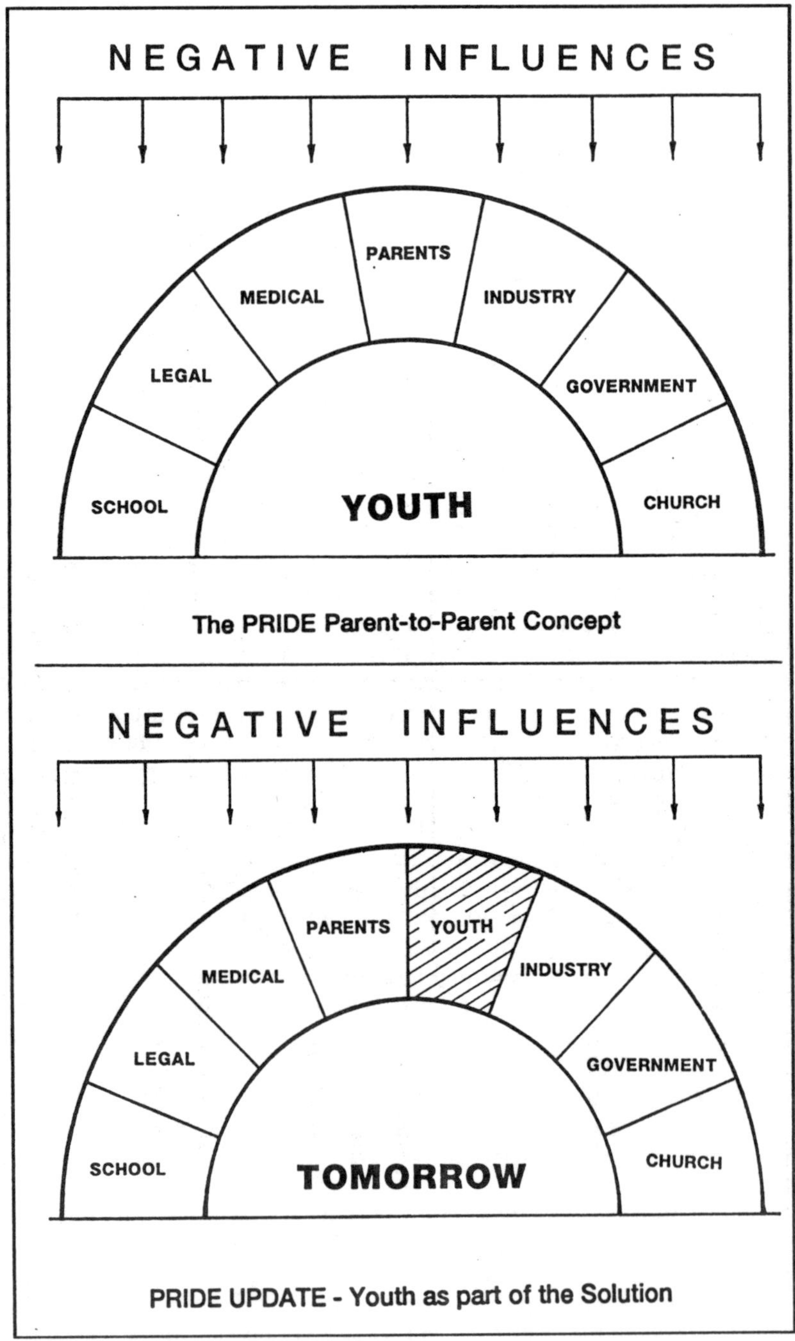


**Figure 4.2 The Protective Arches**

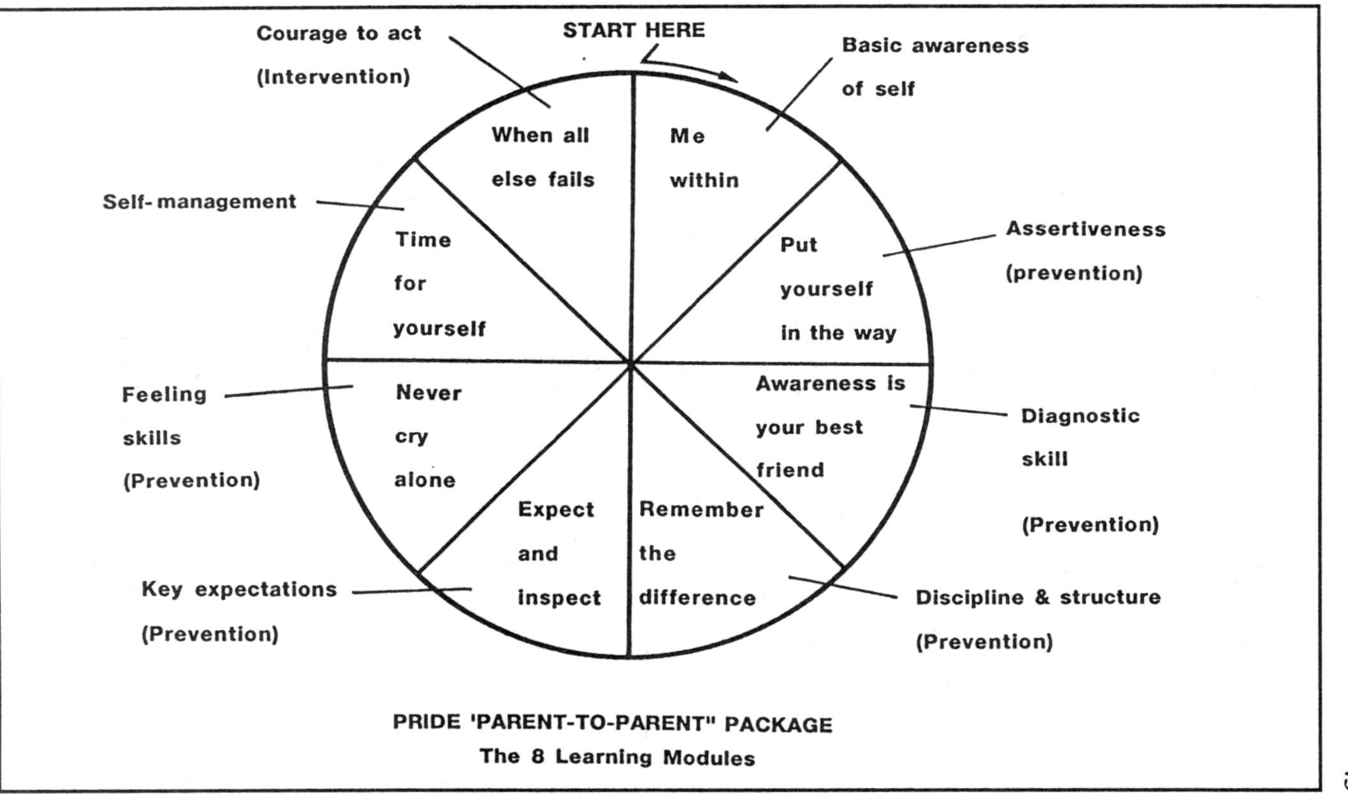


**Figure 4.3 Pride 'Parent-to-Parent' Program**

Philosophy goes on to state that "the most innovative and effective helpers for parents who are trying to cope with adolescent drug and drinking problems are other parents - other adults who have experienced similar difficulties or who want to prevent similar situations from arising".

A former high flyer with IBM and sometime director of youth drug rehabilitation programmes (a serious gap in Britain's treatment spectrum - we have no such programmes) is Bill Oliver. Bill has been instrumental in developing PRIDE's Parent-to-Parent Program.

This is an eight x one hour multi-media package. An hour is considered to be the optimum time for a parent workshop if one is to avoid boring, scaring or confusing them. Each one hour module is structured to allow:

| | | |
|---|---|---|
| 5 minutes | Uncover | Arouse curiosity |
| 30 minutes | Discover | Teach |
| 15 minutes | Recover | Recapitulate |
| 10 minutes | Rest | Short pauses |

The package emphasises the importance of family belief systems. It covers basic drug awareness, awareness of self, family structure, parenting skills, prevention and intervention (if your prevention was too little or too late), behavioural awareness, assertiveness by the parent, discipline and structure, goal-setting, feelings and how to interrelate on this level, being gentle with yourself, and a few items more besides. Figure 4.3 gives a graphical summary of the programme modules.

In common with several other programmes, PRIDE will not sell Parent-to-Parent unless at least two people from a community commit to attending a training, so that they will feel "ownership" and more effectively transmit their learning to others. The alternative "sell to anyone" approach quite often just adds another item to a dusty shelf in a storeroom.

## Snowballs and Snowflakes

Far to the north of Atlanta is the state of Illinois. Eighteen years ago the Illinois Teenage Institute (ITI) was formed and became a national award-winning project which every year newly reaches more than a thousand young people. ITI was in fact the model for the formation of the National Association of Teen Institutes, headquartered in St Louis, Missouri, all of which use the TI Model of a residential prevention experience. The ITI programme is administered by IADDA, the Illinois Alcoholism and Drug Dependency Association, which is strongly involved in prevention as well as treatment.

Week-long camps of 300 or more youth plus a high ratio of adult staff and teen leaders (around 3:1) are assembled. Staff and leaders have received prior training. The whole of the week's activities is conducted on the chosen site. Activity is kept at a high pace throughout, from early morning until late at night, and across a diverse range of subjects germane to prevention. The ITI definition of prevention is worth examination:

> "A pro-active process which empowers individuals and systems to meet the challenges of life events and transitions by creating and reinforcing conditions that promote healthy behavior and lifestyles".

The camp population is sociometrically divided into Discussion Groups which stay together for any Group sessions in the week, during waking hours. Besides whole-camp and Discussion Group work there are subject-based workshops from which the individual may choose. Dormitories, being single sex, require different groupings but even here structured group work is effected; calm reflection on the day's events before lights out.

A brief scanning of the staff handbooks shows the close attention to detailed planning as well as the richness of the programme. Adult and teen staff are given very detailed guidelines in the 150 page handbook. Clear role specifications are given for each category of participant, including warnings as to sessions known in the past to have produced a volatile atmosphere - "Life is a Process" and "It's a Wonderful Life" are two such valuable but knife-edge sessions.

The need for staff to not press their own religious/moral values on participants is emphasised, as is the need to not experiment with counselling. The majority of teens at ITI have no serious emotional baggage which needs attention, and the majority of sessions are therefore geared towards "helping healthy teens stay healthy" and not designed to "open up strong emotions, expose scars or unhealed wounds". Sessions are expected to end on a positive note and there are no sessions where crying is "encouraged". It is not appropriate for staff to "probe" or "break through denial or defenses" during ITI. An important parameter is that healthy teens (who are the majority at ITI) should not be made to feel they are somehow incomplete because they don't have big problems they can parade before the group. Of course, if a teen is found to have substantial problems not previously known but which have come to the surface through the caring, sharing, safe environment of ITI, then specialised help is quickly at hand through the professionals attached to the organisation.

Staff too are vulnerable to some emotional undercutting in this environment, and even within the guidelines for self-disclosure they may find problems suddenly trip them up. Supervision for staff is extensively provided. Another aspect relevant to any residential environment such as this is the potential for romantic attachments to develop between teens, or staff, or teens/staff. The atmosphere (similarly as Open University Summer Schools and the like) is not real life, and a rosy view of one's fellows can become inflated in the "high positive stress" of growth groups into something unsustainable on return to the real world. People can get hurt.

Looking now at the actual activities, the finely-detailed scope can be judged from the fact that fully 40 pages of the manual are given over to one day's work. The day-to-day themes are as follows:

| | |
|---|---|
| SUNDAY | We get to know each other and begin talking about prevention. |
| MONDAY | We work on communicating, learn about addiction and meet people from our "neighborhood" (our area of the camp)<br>We also talk about relationships and gain new insight about ourselves, our families, our family culture, and our peer culture. |
| TUESDAY | We concentrate on specific prevention programs to start (or join) in our communities after ITI, and talk about our life successes - the skills we are proud to have gained. |
| WEDNESDAY | We look at our personal wellness and how to help others. We increase our skills to carry the prevention message to others. |
| THURSDAY | We begin to give the prevention message to the Illinois Government, and start changing the social climate of Illinois. |

A typical day's schedule is given by the listing for Tuesday:

| | |
|---|---|
| 0630 | Staff meeting - review today's activities, answer queries and discuss concerns. |
| 0730-0800 | Breakfast |
| 0815-0845 | Sunrise Sharing and Self Help Meeting. |
| 0900-1000 | Mini Workshops on "Relationships" (pick one). (Encourage participants to develop insight, practise decision- making, examine self-concept and learn how to make low - risk choices):<br>- Refusal Skills and Self-Image<br>- Take a Risk and Come to this Workshop<br>- The Relationship Puzzle, Where Do I Fit In?<br>- Games People Play in Relationships<br>- Everything You Need to Know to Tell Your Peers about AIDS or STDs<br>- Teen Pregnancy and Peer Helping<br>- Moving Your Feet to a Different Beat (Multi-Cultural Sensitivity)<br>- Stages of Relationships<br>- How to Help a Peer Who Falls into a Co-dependency Relationship |

| | |
|---|---|
| 1015-1115 | DISCUSSION GROUP. Discussion No. 4 |
| 1130-1230 | GENERAL SESSION:<br>"Teenagers are People Too"<br>"Where do We Go From Here?"<br>(Think about successful programs you know that depend on teens) |
| 1230-1300 | LUNCH |
| 1315-1415 | GENERAL SESSION:<br>Prevention Overview, Concepts, Strategies, the role of youth |
| 1430-1545 | MINI WORKSHOPS: "Skill Building" (pick one)<br>(Participants will be actively involved in practising new skills, to encourage positive risk-taking. Plan to reinforce these skills when in Discussion Group):<br>- Operation Snowball<br>- Operation Snowflake<br>- Peers Drink-Drive Prevention<br>- ALPHA (Peer-Teaching)<br>- Life-Savers<br>- Multi-Cultural Prevention Programme<br>- Natural Helpers<br>- Teens Preventing AIDS<br>- Adults Introduction to Prevention<br>- How to Work with Kids |
| 1545-1730 | Neighborhood Activities<br>(Help with drifters, lonelies and couples. Assist with organized activities) |
| 1730-1815 | DINNER |
| 1815-1915 | GENERAL SESSION:<br>"Taking Charge of Your Life: It's a Wonderful Life".<br>(Watch for your Discussion Group members' reactions to the stories people give, watch for emotions likely to come up. Listen for positive and inspiring anecdotes) |
| 1945-2100 | DISCUSSION GROUP. Discussion No. 5 |
| 2100-2230 | Pool Party and Other Fun Things |
| 2230 | Room Check. Encourage participants to write their journals. Share positive poems and songs |
| 2300 | Lights Out (**not** negotiable) |

Reference in the above schedule to Operations Snowball and Snowflake links to the title of this piece. This week-long TI will certainly be very impactful, as with any residential experience, but for sustained effect and for continued growth of the participants it needs to be set into an ongoing year-round programme. This is provided by a family of programmes named:

| | |
|---|---|
| Operation Snowflurry | Pre-school and primary age |
| Operation Snowflake | Middle and primary age |
| Operation Snowball | Secondary age |
| Operation Segue | Young adults |
| Operation Blizzard | Adults and families |
| Operation Snowcap | Senior Citizens |

There are more than 80 accredited chapters of the Snowball family in Illinois, Iowa, Indiana and Wisconsin; youth and adults together in positive partnership.

## Best Western

If PRIDE represents the highest standards of programmes from the Southern States and ITI carries the flag for the north, then surely the pride of place in the west must belong to the Tribes process.

Tribes comes out of California but is now used by many other states in widely varying cultures and multi-cultural settings. It has been employed very successfully in England, in several primary and secondary schools in a West London borough. The title "Tribes" is not an acronym, it epitomises the process approach which is to build and nurture "small families". Tribes is a **process**, not a programme, and this is particularly significant for hard-pressed British teachers who are defeated already in trying to accommodate all the subjects and activities various people would like them to cover. Because Tribes is a process it does not require extra classroom time; it will in fact assist the current classroom activities, in that classroom time will (on the evidence of evaluations over many years) become less stressed, and so will the teaching staff. The underlying principle for Tribes is a technology called Co-operative Learning. In 1974 when Tribes was at a seminal stage Co-operative Learning was also starting to emerge as a technology; research on the ground was starting to validate pupils working in perpetuated small groups to tackle academic tasks and to develop social skills through co-operation in their group.

The researchers at the Center for Human Development (CHD) in California were aware of Co-operative Learning as an option in their design of solutions to several major problems, viz:

- Declining academic grades
- Increased behaviour problems, truancy, drop-out, delinquency, teen pregnancy, suicides, and alcohol/drug

abuse
- Increased teacher burn-out/drop-out

CHD also looked at the problems children were themselves experiencing. This is, if you like, a deficiency model for observations, but none the less valid for that. The researchers found:

- Low self-esteem
- Anti-social behaviours; lying, teasing, fighting
- Disrespect of teachers
- Lack of motivation
- Apathy, depression and alienation
- Low reading scores
- Work quality generally deteriorating

In the face of pressure to return to the 3Rs (does any of this sound familiar to you in Britain?) the CHD researchers consulted ERIC (Educational Research Information Clearinghouse). Firstly, correlates were sought with individual academic achievement and problem behaviours, and they found:

- Direct correlations of self-esteem to reading scores
- Correlation of low self-image to low achievement and behaviour problems
- Anti-social behaviour in young children predicts early use of alcohol and/or drugs
- External loss of control in adolescents correlates to juvenile delinquency
- Direct correlation of teachers' and peers' negative perceptions of academic ability to arithmetic achievement

Good news was also given by ERIC, in the form of correlates with positive outcomes:

- Positive peer regard improves self-image
- Co-operative learning methods lead to higher test scores
- A positive classroom climate enhances motivation and improves behaviour

It is noteworthy that none of these correlates has anything to do with "deficiency" in individuals.

The CHD researchers also consulted other experts in the field, including the distinguished Professor Dr Benjamin S. Bloom of the University of Chicago, best known for his "system of taxonomy for learning". Bloom found that in the 20,000 hours or so that a student spends in school, only a small percentage of time addresses the "latent" curriculum of social interactions. Bloom questions which of the two curricula will leave a more affective impression ... the maths lesson or:

- The humility of being an isolate
- The fear of being teased
- The confusion of feelings unexpressed
- A feeling of powerlessness when pressured by peers
- The ways that decisions are made and rules enforced
- The partiality of a teacher towards other students

**HOW TIMES HAVE CHANGED**

The top seven discipline problems in public school in the 1940s and the top seventeen problems in the 1980s:

| **1940s** | **1980** |
|---|---|
| 1. Talking | 1. Drug abuse |
| 2. Chewing gum | 2. Alcohol abuse |
| 3. Making noise | 3. Pregnancy |
| 4. Running in the halls | 4. Suicide |
| 5. Getting out of turn in line | 5. Rape |
| 6. Wearing improper clothing | 6. Robbery |
| 7. Not putting paper in wastebaskets | 7. Assault |
| | 8. Burglary |
| | 9. Arson |
| | 10. Bombings |
| | 11. Murder |
| | 12. Absenteeism |
| | 13. Vandalism |
| | 14. Extortion |
| | 15. Gang warfare |
| | 16. Abortion |
| | 17. Venereal disease |

Author's Note, 1992:
N.B. absence of HIV/AIDS, sexual abuse, and racism.

**Figure 4.4 Problems Over the Years**

Pulling these and other strands together CHD started to formulate a positive initiative around classroom environment, peer relationships, social behaviour, and teaching methods. Humanistic psychology drawn from Maslow, Adler, Rogers and others was the basis. The Deficiency Model (i.e. identify a symptom, do a localised repair, send it back into service) was rejected outright, as ignoring the environment/s which had produced the behaviour in the first instance. CHD's approach was to tackle the environment so that the symptoms would not appear. This is a total match with William Lofquist's work for Associates for Youth Development, Arizona, and set down in his classic 1983 text "Discovering the Meaning of Prevention" (see Chapter 6).

Whilst the CHD researchers were looking at all forms of behaviour in both the academic and the social arenas, they were very conscious of the particular significance of drug abuse. A survey of teachers across the United States in the 1940s and again in the 1980s (source unknown) produced the a graphic comparison of the school environment as perceived by the teachers. They were asked to list what they saw as the major discipline problems in school, and Figure 4.4 is what they came up with.

Drug abuse and alcohol abuse, first and second on the hit parade. A strong indicator to CHD workers now moving out of research and into development. For none of the CHD staff was this more true than founder Jeanne Gibbs. Jeanne's son Dave spent many years addicted to drugs, before winning his personal battle and training to become a staff member for CHD, in charge of the "NEAT program" which uses a mix of self-help and facilitation groups to help using adolescents get themselves clean and stay that way.

Jeanne took the synethesis of research and development by the CHD staff and translated it into the Tribes program. Pilot testing in many classrooms by CHD in association with the teachers honed the programme into its final shape.

## Essence of the Programme

Applicable to any age group up to and including senior citizens, Tribes is used mostly in primary schools and then in secondary schools. A teacher will spend the whole of the first term (and maybe longer) getting to know her class and observing the leaders, followers, isolates, disrupters, etc. She will also run several academic or other tasks in couples, trios, quartets, etc., and observe how these work. From this basis she will then form sociometrically (gender-race-ability-personality, etc.) balanced Tribes of around 5 or 6 youths. If her groundwork has been sound there should be little need to switch members between Tribes, and the aim is to have a student stay in the same Tribe for as long as the schooling structure (streaming, etc.) allows.

A first task is to discuss and agree the behavioural norms for the Tribe. The norms are as shown in Figure 4.5. One can argue that greater "ownership" is achieved if the Tribe develops its own norms, but for the group process to operate effectively, all the norms as listed have to be included in any greater list a group may develop. In any case, these norms are typical of groupwork in this context; any self-help or rehabilitation group uses much the same ground rules, and for a further current example

Page 8 of CG5 (Curriculum Guidance 5: National Curriculum Council) shows what a group of 11-year olds came up with. The younger the group the more guidance is needed, but with older groups there remains the need to ensure that group dynamics are not jeopardised by ignorant or wilful omission of any of the sound and scientifically derived norms published by Tribes.

The power of these norms is such that even if the rest of the programme is not followed, working to these norms produces benefits in behaviour and relationships which may well reflect in improved performance later. The "right to pass on any subject" has wider value; whilst it permits a student to remain silent on a subject (such as death, parent problems, etc.) which are contemporarily painful, at a prosaic level it enables you to avoid the stress crescendo experienced as the facilitator works round the circle towards you and what you had rehearsed has already been "stolen" by previous speakers. Lastly and most significantly, the student learns it is "OK to say no" amongst peers, without challenge - a valuable experiential lesson for later, in the playground or the street.

**Figure 4.5 Tribes - group norms of behaviour**

The class will perform many of its academic tasks in Tribes groups, and English schools which have used it have reported it fits very well with the National Curriculum. Exercises are offered for use during such as PSE (Personal and Social Education) or Citizenship lessons, and it is of great value to have short periods of "Tribe Time", when students can share thoughts and feelings with each other in the trusting atmosphere which quickly develops. Lessons are structured to engender a progression from Inclusion to Influence to Affection. That is, students start by feeling they are members of a community before the main business i.e. learning, and conclude by validating and appreciating their own performance and that of their colleagues. Inclusion may come from a Community Circle involving the whole class, or be in Tribes. Similarly with validation and appreciation.

The downstream benefits of Tribes are most encouraging. Drug/alcohol abuse is reduced, but so is delinquency, vandalism, bullying, racism and more. However, for those schools who are in heavy denial as to what is going on with their pupils (and such denial will be exacerbated by Local Management of Schools and the need to "market" the school) the other observed benefits of Tribes may strike a more welcome chord. They are:

- Improved class discipline
- Smoother classroom management
- Reduced non-attendance
- Better teacher-pupil relations
- Better parent-pupil relations, and
- Improved academic performance!

Therefore, if you want to sell the idea of Tribes to your headmaster, you may be better advised to start by highlighting these rewards, judiciously leaving mentioning the spin-off of drug prevention for another day.

Like many programmes, Tribes relates purchase of the training materials to the completion of a basic training course. This is now available in England and is tailored to match the realities of National Curriculum structures, supply teacher limitations, etc.

**And Moreover ...**

Many other wonderful prevention organisations and programmes have been visited by the author in the United States; enough to fill several books like this. Organisations like Prevention Plus of Morrow, Georgia; working face-to-face with low-income kids. Youth to Youth from Ohio (slogan "My Choice - Drug Free") but operating extensively in many states, in work similar to ITI and also mounting major youth conferences with large attendances. The NFPDFY, National Federation of Parents for Drug-Free Youth which correlates the activities of 8,000 parents groups across America. The DEA Sports Drug Awareness Programs using clean sports heroes/heroines as role models. The DARE program (Drug Abuse Resistance Education) in which trained police officers go into elementary grade schools and give a very extensive and sustained training - not the 'one-off' dissuader visit we often get in Britain; DARE officers give 17 two-hour lessons to each year class! They also spend a day a week in the school, eat and relax with the kids so that they become part of the scenery. (Chapter 12 says more on DARE, see "The Case for the Law"). Narcotics and Drug Research Inc. of New York, the second largest resource centre (after NIDA) in the US. NIDA (National Institute on Drug Abuse) is not confined to prevention but covers all drug matters fully from its Washington DC offices. OSAP, The Office of Substance Abuse Prevention also based in Washington DC is, as its name suggests, more focused in its aims. And last but by no means least the Just Say No clubs of America. Lampooned by the media and pro-drug groups in Britain, Just Say No became the convenient catchphrase to reinforce prejudice about Americans in general and Nancy Reagan in particular, for what was perceived to be a superficial campaign based on mindless incantation by the young of this simplistic catchphrase. The reality is very different: Just Say No clubs pursue a broad and full programme of drug awareness, skill-building, prevention and social activities with a competency that would put many a British Health Education specialist to shame. There is certainly more to Just Say No than just saying no.

**Business Matters - The EAP**

Prevention is a community matter, and businesses are an important, vital part of the community. Whilst the first assumption as to the role of business in prevention is that they are potential fund-givers, the full picture is much wider than that.

Members of businesses - white or blue collar - are just as open to temptation of drug abuse as anyone else, moreover not a few of them will be partners (of whatever sexual orientation) or parents, or both. For these reasons the business arena is one in which prevention workers should be major players.

In America businesses interrelate with general community prevention, for example they will invite specialist speakers to talk at "brown bag" lunches; the company provides a free bagged lunch for anyone attending the talk. Businesses also join in the National Red Ribbon Week in which the wearing of or decking out with red ribbons signifies commitment to drug-free life. But the single largest commitment comes in the form of EAPs - Employee Assistance Programs. These started life as strictly reactive measures and mainly confined to alcohol problems in the workforce, but soon matured into much more, and now give guidance and assistance with primary prevention either within the workforce or for the families of the workforce. The pharmaceuticals giant, Johnson & Johnson published results in early 1992 of their Wellness (Health Promotion) programme. These results showed a 2 for 1 return on investment ($200 spent produced $400 savings per person). Because Wellness programmes spend money on all employees, not just problem people, the return on investment is lower than problem-focused EAPs. This evolution from Workplace Alcohol Policy to EAP to Health Promotion is something which has yet to happen in Britain; indeed most companies have not yet taken the first step.

Several lessons were learnt by the Americans in this evolution. One could provide the necessary alcohol or drug counselling through having an outside agency called in on demand, or by sending the worker to the agency. A better arrangement was to have a surgery on site, full time if a large company, shared with other companies if not. However, this person needed to be **not on the payroll**; bad experiences of pressurising counsellors to reveal information to employers were a risk otherwise. Moreover, having a room known to be the "Alcohol Problem Room" meant that many would refuse to enter, under the eyes of colleagues. Partly for this pragmatic reason, but also because of increasing recognition of the prevention potential, the scope was widened to Employee Assistance, covering finance, mortgages, law, children's education, matrimonial disputes, anxiety and stress, family behavioural problems and (by the way) alcohol and drug matters pending or current. This way no one could know if an employee was visiting to discuss his mortgage, his wife, or his drug of choice. This widening meant that back-up from specialised advisors had to be on tap, but it greatly increased the throughput on the schemes, and moved closer to a prevention, i.e. environment-improved approach, away from the reactive, i.e. deficit-model approach.

There is a wealth of literature on the subject of EAPs and their second-division cousin, ECS - Employee Counselling Services. Dr Dale Masi of the University of Maryland is a leading authority on the subject.

Rounding out this brief dissertation on the resources available in America to the prevention student, a firm recommendation is for attendance at one or more PRIDE International Conferences. Contact PRIDE for details, at the Hurt Building, Suite 210, 50 Hurt Plaza, Atlanta, Georgia 30303, USA. (Tel: 404-577-4500, Fax: 404-688-6937).

**Australians Give a XXXX**

The stereotype image of the beer-swilling, macho, cork-dangling Aussie has done the country significant damage. Australian lagers have done not a little damage themselves, but one cannot blame the producer so much as the consumer for this, and it was interesting in this context to read reports of uproar at Bondi Beach on Christmas Day 1991 in which shocked Australians watched the ruckus being caused, mostly by drunken Britons.

Australia has in fact been very active in response to drug use, and has much to be proud of in the areas of intervention, outreach, treatment, education and training, and prevention. The prevention initiative most Britons will be familiar with is the Life Education Centre. LEC's mobile classrooms first came into this country under the dual sponsorship of TV

AM and the Dire Straits rock band, and there are now several mobiles covering primary schools across the country. The idea was conceived under the inspirational stewardship of the Reverend Ted Noffs in Sydney, Australia in the early 1980s. Reverend Ted ran the Wayside Chapel in Sydney, not just a church but also a Crisis Centre; from the 1960s he was involved in schools drug education and he found both in his own work and that of others worldwide that drug education was typified by its scarcity, erratic quality and evasion. "Generally" says Ted (in 1983) "the situation can best be described as one of studied neglect. Increasingly teachers feel it is not their role to educate young people specifically on this subject. The problem is too controversial". The LEC has proved to be a very constructive response to this condition of chronic myopia, and is now a valued part of Australia's drug prevention repertoire.

The mobile classroom, some 30 feet long, can be fed from two conventional 13 amp plugs or from a small generator. The interior is carpetted with soundproofing, sophisticated lighting, audio and visual systems. Backlit screens supplement video. A life-size transparent manikin lights up in different sections to indicate the various systems of the body. Glove puppets give a humorous delivery to the lessons, which start by exploring the body, how it works, and what happens when you put various foods or other substances into it. From this basis the lessons can graduate to study of drug use and also to consideration of other health issues such as diet, exercise and HIV/AIDS.

An important requirement of a school is that the LEC visit should **not** be a "circus visit", to be forgotten a few days later. Teachers obtain the workbooks weeks earlier and do preparatory work leading up to the actual visit, which can be shared between several schools. After the visit there are further classroom exercises and the children also have the opportunity to join the Harold Club (Harold being the giraffe glove puppet who features in many of the stories), receiving the occasional journal, the Harold.

LEC workers have a wide range of activities they can resource and provide literature for, which can be designed into the teacher's longer term curriculum.

## Christie, Wal and Tiddles

Australia, like Britain and America, has been experiencing pressure for years to legalise drugs including cannabis and heroin, with the AIDS crisis adding fuel to the fire. In Sydney the most popular drug is Ecstasy, in line with the London "rave" scene. After almost ten years of producing message books which were humorous rather than hectoring, Terry Watt was asked to produce a pack specific to drug/alcohol abuse.

The result was the Kangaroo Creek Gang, a multi-media pack which can be used in the classroom or (by parents) at home or in the community. With 50:50 funding from Government and Mercantile Mutual, a major insurance company, it was possible to give a free copy to all 8,000 primary schools across the country. Initial territorial resistance to having one package for the whole country (the perennial bugbear of educator conceit) was overcome by the promise of the above-mentioned major business funding if agreement was reached, and by involving all six State Health Education workers in the production.

The core of the programmes is the correlation between avoidance of negative behaviours and the Enhancement of Self. Thus, the healthier your self-concept is, the less need there is to take drugs ... The more aware an individual is of total self, the healthier is the self-concept, comprising the attitudes and beliefs one holds of self ("I am a person who ...") has its origins in the assumptions one holds of self ("Am I a person who ...?"). The development of a healthy self-concept involves the testing-out of these assumptions and simultaneously receiving feedback from "significant others" about the testing out of the assumptions. Teachers' and parents' key responsibility in the enhancement of children's self-concept is to accept the role of "significant others". The relationship between drug education and self-concept is linked to the degree an individual knows, understands and values self. The more an individual knows and values self, the healthier is their communication of self to others and the more prepared they are to say "No" when confronted with peer group pressure. The more an individual knows, understands and values self, the less need he/she has to resort to communications substitutes and the less need there is to take drugs, alcohol, analgesics when communicating self to others.

Within a hardback ring binder is a 150-page teachers' training resource, a video giving two stories, and an audio giving songs and dance music. Glove puppets for all the main characters are also available as an optional extra. The audio tape also gives a briefing on the whole package for parents and introduces the 45-page parents' handbook, for use in the home setting.

The video is the focal point of the programme, just as the mobile classroom is with LEC. The video tells two stories. The first, "Feeling Prickly" is for younger primary-age pupils, but is used also as a forerunner to the second story, "The Real Kangaroo" for middle/upper primary ages. Used selectively, this latter story can even be presented to Year 7/8 secondary pupils. For example, one can say "This video is starting to be used in primary schools. If you were that age, what would you get out of it?". In fact, the video has been used in this focused context for adult trainings.

"Feeling Prickly" tells of Eddie, a porcupine who "doesn't like himself, so he thinks nobody else likes him". Shunning the gang, he stays up late watching TV (including pharmaceutical adverts). When feeling rough the following morning he presses the vet for medication but learns that for him the answer is "mostly around you but also inside you". Another animal does need medication but is carefully briefed on how to use it. Eddie learns that we all have something special we can celebrate, and that unbending enough to trust those who show friendship and seem unaffected by what we see as our failings can bring big dividends.

In the second story "The Real Kangaroo", Kelly is orphaned and brought up (as does happen sometimes) by a human family until "adolescence". She becomes too large for human habitat and leaves the comfort of home and family to discover the outside world. There are friendly souls to be found, the Kangaroo Creek Gang, who caution her against risks (whilst sometimes considering themselves old enough to take a few). One day Kelly encounters two streetwise kangaroos who introduce her to the thrills of risky living. She is desperate to show her worth to them by taking any risk they specify. However, when they "get into Blue Moss" she remembers the Gang's admonition to avoid this unhealthy substance and fakes using it. It is only after several subsequent thrills and disasters that she seeks out the moss and uses it. Eventually Libby Lizard acts as a small voice in Kelly's ear to guide her to reviewing her decisions; not to defend earlier decisions by repeating them, but to take new decisions based on today's scene. Also not to "beat herself up" about past mistakes or perceived inadequacies, but to look forward positively. The story closes with her seeking out the streetwise kangaroos again, but this time taking the initiative herself by inviting them to "Come over to my place and meet the Gang".

As well as the activities directly related to the stories there are Extension Activities which can either be used as supplementary work or can stand on their own merit.

## The Australasian Axis

While PRIDE has been the driving force in the Western World there has been no lack of effort in the East. The INFNGO - International Federation of Non-Governmental Organisations has been in operation for almost as long, and will be holding its 14th Annual Conference in 1992. Conferences are for professional practitioners rather than parents/youth/community and as such they do not attract the enormous numbers of PRIDE, nevertheless attendances of 500 or more practitioners from more than 30 countries make this a major forum.

A sample of the papers presented at INFNGO Conferences (this author attended in 1987) gives some idea of the calibre of this organisation:

The Abuse of Psychotropic Substances in Japan
Dr Masaaki Kato, Tokyo Medical College
How Regional NGOs can Work Together in Drug Abuse
RC. Hon. Dato Rais Yatim, Malaysia
Community Participation in Developing Responses to Alcohol Problems
Marvin Burke, Nova Scotia, Canada
Prevention Strategies in the Phillipines
Sofia Q. Quejas, Manila, Phillipines
Prevention; a Revolution in Attitude
K.L. Stumpf, Kowloon, Hong Kong
The Wayside Chapel's Prevention Education Program
Rev. Ted Noffs, Sydney, Australia

Community-based Prevention Programs in Australia
Pierre Stolz, Canberra, Australia
Aspects of Spirituality in San Pedro Peninsula Hospital
Fr. Leo Booth, California, USA
A Comparison of the Efficacy and Tolerability of Clobazam and Chlordiazepoxide in the Treatment of Acute Withdrawal from Alcohol in Patients with Primary Alcoholism
Dr P.K. Mukherjee, Airdrie, Scotland

Dr Mukherjee's paper was notable not only for the length of its title but also for his being the only speaker that year from the United Kingdom. Said Kingdom is also conspicuous by its absence at PRIDE conferences; the average attendance over the last five years has been below three, in a typical conference population of over 7,000. Some would argue that this shows that Britain is behind the game, insular, and with much catching up to do. Others, however, are quite capable of arguing that it shows Britain has nothing to learn from other countries, and it is everyone else who is out of step. You are invited to draw your own conclusion.

**Europe Starts to Catch Up**

If Britain has been largely absent from PRIDE conferences, other European nations (and neighbours) have not. There has always been a sizeable contingent, large enough for a European Delegates Group to be formed in 1988.

Delegates from Portugal, Spain, Belgium, Italy, Eire, Switzerland, England, Germany, Czechoslovakia, Poland, Sweden, Norway, Finland and Iceland formed ad-hoc groups to pass resolutions, and in some discussions were joined by others from "further east", such as Greece, Cyprus, Turkey, India, Pakistan and Nepal.

At the 1989 Conference European delegates heard of the scandalous situation in Switzerland, where legalisation was being steamrollered by small but well-organised pressure groups such as "Swiss Friends of Pot" and "Physicians for Psychedelics". Their demands were for legalisation of cannabis and psychedelics, plus free access to pure heroin and pure cocaine. The media printed acres of pro-drug coverage but usually spiked prevention submissions; TV seemed to operate to the same bias. The European Group at PRIDE drafted, agreed and signed a strong resolution condemning this situation and reminding Switzerland of its commitment to the UN Single Convention, concluding with prevention recommendations. The Latin American Group also countersigned the resolution and it received the strongest possible endorsement when Dr Gleaton put it to the whole conference assembly where it received unanimous approval.

The situation in Switzerland remains messy and distressing. News reports in January 1992 described the ending of "a bold sociological experiment". For four years a riverside park in Zurich was designated as a police-free Harm Reduction area. Drug users were allowed to deal and use. Food and needles were distributed, as many as 12,000 needles per day. Dealers commuted from Turkey and the Lebanon, but most users were indigenous. It was not a pretty sight. Three or four users died each night. Thousands of syringes littered the ground. Crime rose enormously. Volunteers took on a haunted look. After four years of hoping to improve the lot of users the experiment was called off, and the users dispersed to hostels around the city. If this was another facet of the War on Drugs, then it was a battle with no winners.

If the impression is gained from PRIDE conferences that Europeans are tagging onto the technological coat-tails of their American counterparts, this is in part because it is true, but also undoubtedly derives from the awe that such a massive happening generates. The International Conference is in any case small in numbers compared to the overall event, and of course European delegates face higher travelling costs than North/South American colleagues. Even so, there have been substantial if isolated presentations of quality from European delegates.

On their home ground the Europeans come into their own, and late 1991 saw the emergence of the first European consortium dedicated to primary prevention. On the eastern margin of Belgium, close to the German border lies the province of the German-speaking Belgian community, centred on the cities of Eupen and St Vith. Its total population is less than 70,000. Despite this small population base the province has a drug/alcohol response network to be proud of, much of which can be attributed to one man. For more than twelve years Ernst Servais has practised in the Social-Psychological Centre (SPZ) at Eupen which also runs counselling centres in Eupen and St Vith. During that time he and his colleagues have developed, piloted, refined and now published practical approaches to drug prevention which can be readily understood by the lay practitioner. The collation of his work is contained in his book published in 1991 in four languages (English, French, Hungarian and German). The English version is called "Before it's too late" - a sentiment many prevention workers would wish to endorse.

In October of 1991 Ernst's centre organised a select working conference of European accredited practitioners, as a precursor to a major international conference (during 1992). 1991 delegates represented the European Commission, Luxembourg, Poland, Hungary, Portugal, France, the three provinces of Belgium (French, German, and Flemish-speaking) Germany (both halves) and Britain (including this author). Somewhat peculiarly, there was also a delegation from Quebec; they had been liaising with France and Belgium for years, and evidently felt more affinity with Europe than with their English-speaking Canadian countrymen. Their inclusion was nevertheless most valuable in giving another cultural perspective from a people having roots in Europe.

It was evident from the contributions to the plenary and workshop sessions that many European countries are a good way down the road to effective prevention. They understand that education alone is not enough, that a process approach is needed which encompasses education, attitudes and behavioural matters, is cognisant of the effects of environment and systems around the person, and involves the person themselves participatively in a holistic prevention strategy.

There are differences in emphasis between countries but essentially all are pointing in the same direction. Several countries gave presentations of their prevention models which were heartening in the degree of development and sophistication they showed. Certainly several are further on than Britain, with Portugal and Belgium as two immediate examples.

## Portugal

In Portugal much of the prevention effort is spearheaded by a unit coming under the Minister for Youth. Projecto Vida has as its slogan "For a Life Filled with Purpose". Vida also runs intervention and treatment and rehabilitation centres; this has the spin-off that prevention workers are not out of touch with the reality of drug use. A vigorous and well-trained corps of workers having youthwork or related skills is involved throughout Portugal in a variety of community-based prevention programmes, with positive alternative activity as a cornerstone of their strategies. Vida have developed their own "Parent-to-Parent" programme which has been enthusiastically adopted by parents across the country, in rural and urban areas.

The basis of the programme is to "pyramid-train" parents, the training cascading from Vida central workers outwards to parents in general. Once basic training has allowed parents to recognise that they are not powerless in this situation, that they have a valid contribution to make, and that they are in fact key players ("Teachers are important but parents are more important" - Dr Maria das Dores Formosinho, University of Coimbra) then they rapidly become a potent group of workers. There are now several hundred of them and they are considering forming their own NGO (Non-Governmental Organisation).

To equip their youth for personal enjoyment of a drug-free life and to facilitate peer teaching and peer leadership to the same end, Projecto Vida has adopted an English programme, Teenex (see Chapter 5). Vida could not translate "Teenex" into Portugese, so they called it "Jovem-a-Jovem" (Youth to Youth). Between Christmas 1989 and October 1991 Vida had run no less than 21 "Teenex" prevention camps, each involving some 50 young people and 6 facilitators. Like the parents movement, these 1000 plus youth are keen to develop their own organisation, but their ambitions extend further to making the youth organisation international.

Vida's other preventive strategies include a cadre of 31 specially trained teachers who between them cover some 280 schools across Portugal, organising activities with pupils, parents, fellow-teachers and other staff, and the community around the school. They also ensure that prevention, which is integrated into the curricula for all between age 6 and 15, is actually put into practice. Vida also organises debates, workshops, trainings and conferences for specialised or generic groups throughout the nation. Vida is not self-serving in that it is happy to encourage new or existing groups to take up the issues. A 24-hour helpline and postbag operates seven days a week, and since March 1988 has been averaging 20,000 calls and 10,000 letters a year; it is staffed with specially-trained psychologists and social workers, and offers advice/counselling on prevention, treatment, social integration, leisure activities, professional training, employment, and more. Vida also funds information campaigns: TV commercials usually avoid "drug images" and concentrate on people and positive opportunities; more than 150 newspapers regularly publish copy sent to them by Vida. They produce posters, pamphlets, badges, stickers, balloons - the fully panoply. They produce and distribute free video films to parents and to youth groups. Travelling exhibitions reach yet more of the public. Voluntary sector bodies providing for young people at risk can be grant-aided by Vida. Private enterprise is encouraged to invest in prevention activities for employees. HIV/AIDS is covered in the educational materials, as is sexuality. Vida also assists with the Armed Forces prevention programme. All of this is regularly evaluated.

## Belgium

In the time since 1979 the German Community of Belgium has been able to try and test many strategies and tactics. From the outset it was agreed by the Social-Psychological Centre (SPZ) under Ernst Servais that a multifaceted approach was the only realistic way, matching activity to the various environments in which people live, work, learn, play and socialise. From the first design of a prevention model, field testing was carried out by more than a hundred teachers in fourteen secondary schools; this was supplemented by co-operation between drug workers, educationists, statisticians and others in working groups.

SPZ developed prevention approaches for six areas of life - Nursery/Primary schools, Secondary schools, Home, Community, Workplace and Leisure. Subsequently a seventh sector was defined by SPZ as the Media but this can be considered as part of the Workplace sector if preferred. For each sector a working group of those within it was formed to co-ordinate and facilitate action. Groups were charged with responsibility for staying up to date with "the realities of life in each environment", and with regular effectiveness measurement of the work in their sector. For each sector a five-point sequence of work was defined:

Learning about the background, enquiring about the people in this sector.
Adapting the educational concept and agreeing a common standpoint.
Looking for co-workers; training.
Preparing educational material; staying well-informed.
Checking effectiveness.

As an example of the specialised services developed within each sector, the Home sector included a "School for Parents" formed in 1986; this meets regularly in premises which include a creche. Parents can discuss child-raising problems, receive training and role-play solutions. Three groups of ten are handled at a time.

The principles by which SPZ work; what they call their "pedagogical concept" matches well with other approaches recommended within this publication. SPZ are seeing the benefits of more than ten years of sustained effort. Schools are now much more involved at all age levels, and "have freed themselves from the social isolation where they found themselves in 1979".

**Comparative analyses of 14-18 year olds in 1981 and 1990 show a downward trend in both illegal and legal drug use.**

Parents in discussion groups are now much freer to discuss their own needs, inadequacies, feelings and pressures; no longer confining themselves to a patriarchal review of children's needs. Many adult organisations are now training their members so that they are no longer reliant on visiting "experts".

The German Community of Belgium has undoubtedly contributed greatly to the improved commitment to prevention within Europe. Their Ministry for Social Affairs under Minister Lambertz has pressed the European Community to get involved, and at the 1991 Eupen conference, CELAD (Committee Européen pour Liaison Anti-Drogues) was much in evidence, as were other Commission officials. CELAD has produced a "European Plan to Combat Drugs".

That Britain intends to be a part of this new drive may best be evidenced by the fact that both the Home Office's Central Drug Prevention Unit and the Department of Health's Demand Reduction Task Force sent senior officials to the 1991 Eupen conference. This was in addition to two invited NGO delegates from England.

The awakening has begun.

# CHAPTER 5

# THE BRITISH EXPERIENCE

In the context of promoting drug use, the British continue to have an unenviable reputation. Opium yesterday, alcohol and tobacco today. In the context of responding to it Britain is probably best known for the so-called "British System" of the 60s; the mythological definition of this system goes something like "convince them you're hooked and they'll give you your favourite drug for free". The mythology was enough to start a reverse Gold Rush from the Americas and elsewhere, back to the Old Country. Here is as good a spot as any to set the record straight, drawing from the text of a presentation to the PRIDE 1990 Conference by Michael Snell, the official responsible for drug matters at HM British Embassy in Washington ...

> "Until the 60s medical practitioners had autonomy on treatment of drug dependents, but with few options: 'cold turkey' abstinence, or heroin reduction. From 1924 until the 60s this practise had held good, the number of dependents was small and virtually constant. With the upsurge in heroin use during the 60s, government saw the need to impose tighter controls, including buffering general practitioners from enterprising users and their ingenious ways of extracting bigger 'scrips' (prescriptions). Government decided that only doctors licensed by the Home Secretary could henceforth prescribe heroin (or cocaine), and all users so prescribed had to be registered. In practice, all licensed doctors were specialists in addiction or working under such specialists. During the 70s there was a shift from heroin to the substitute, methadone, with very few remaining on heroin. Heroin prescription is now a treatment of last resort and in 1989 only some 69 addicts were so treated out of a total of 14,785 addicts notified to the Chief Medical Officer".

Britain does not taken an acquiescent line on drug use either. At the 1990 World Ministerial Summit on drug demand reduction the then Prime Minister Margaret Thatcher said:

> "... you can't beat drug-taking by legalising drugs. That is the way to destroy young lives, ruin families, and undermine society itself. Our task is to protect young people, not deliberately expose them to danger. I can assure you that our government will never legalise drugs, hard or soft".

Pro-drug factions would draw a grain of comfort from that last clause; the concept that there may be such a thing as a soft drug has obviously been successfully implanted in the Ministerial Mind.

Preventionists however had much more to be enthusiastic about. Arising from the Summit there came two immediate initiatives, between them constituting the first dedicated ventures in prevention at government level. The Central Drug Prevention Unit (CDPU) comes under the Home Office and is based close to the House of Commons. The stated objective of the CDPU was to establish up to twenty Local Drug Prevention Units (LDPUs) in locations across England, Scotland and Wales. Each of these teams was to have an anticipated three-year term during which time they would "stimulate, harness and reinforce community action against drugs misuse". The units were not to act in isolation from existing services but in a complementary role. Because of this role the teams have the brief not only of primary prevention with non-users but also prevention of progression to heavier use by experimental or occasional users.

Local teams (LDPUs) comprise three full-time staff and have the objectives of raising public awareness, facilitating better co-ordinated prevention efforts, supporting existing agencies to strengthen and extend their prevention work, mobilising other community bodies (parents, teachers, churches, the media) to be active in prevention, and initiating "projects which have the support of community representatives". This last point is a valuable rider on new initiatives; local groups can be jealous of their prerogative and even the best ideas can crash on take-off if this factor is ignored. In part this is covered by having a Local Advisory Group of community interests, statutory and voluntary to oversee and support the work of LDPUs. Each of the twenty teams has £75,000 per year available for grant aid to local prevention work, plus a £10,000 annual budget for publicity-related expenditure.

Thus far, teams have been established in Birmingham, Brighton, Liverpool, Bristol, Newcastle-upon-Tyne, Nottingham, Wolverhampton, and the London Boroughs of Hackney, Newham, Lewisham, Southwark, Brent and Lambeth. At the time of writing this book other teams extant or imminent are Bradford, Dundee, Wirral, Glasgow, Manchester, Salford and West Glamorgan. Twenty in all.

The second initiative to arise from the 1990 World Ministerial Summit was the Demand Reduction Task Force. Based in the Ministry of Health, this unit is intended to be more in the export business than import; its brief is to provide training in Britain's demand reduction expertise to the rest of the world. Missions are starting with former colonies and protectorates for which it is perceived that the British administrative culture may be more naturally understood. The first mission was to Belize. Belize has however had a PRIDE group for more than 10 years; its organisers can and do hold their own amongst the best of PRIDE's consultants; the outcome from this mission will therefore be valuable to both parties, and may set a pattern for useful two- way exchange with each country which the Demand Reduction Task Force visits.

## The Broad Response to Drug Use in Britain

Britain has been no better or worse than America in using a symptom-focused (or deficiency model) approach to drug use, in contrast with the "improve reality" approach which Lofquist and others have for years protagonised. In the early 80s, Government reacted to concern about solvent sniffing by inviting Local Authorities to bid for funds for Drug Education and Intervention. They also enacted legislation making it much harder for youth to buy adhesives, unwittingly pushing the sniffers towards the even more dangerous aerosols. This pump-priming funding brought several new agencies into existence, such as the Substance Abuse Unit in the London Borough of Hillingdon. Counselling and referral services were supplemented by community awareness activities, parent and agency training, and the beginnings of school-based drug education.

However, the real impetus to specialised drug education in schools did not come until 1986, when Government again invited bids for funding, this time for a Drug Education Co-ordinator (DEC), hopefully in every Local Education Authority. Their brief was to promote, guide, co-ordinate and where feasible directly contribute to drug education in the school setting. At a later date, Government advised that DECs should also cover tobacco, alcohol and HIV/AIDS in their scope - for many DECs this was startling, as they always had automatically included these and other essential components in any meaningful drug education package. The DECs developed a strong reputation and Government were pleased to extend their period of funding more than once; as things stand today the DEC sands of time run out in Spring 1993.

## TACADE

Long before DECs were invented schools had one organisation they could rely on for prevention-oriented educational resources. TACADE, founded in 1969, used to be named the Teachers Advisory Council for Alcohol and Drug Education; the acronym now starts **The** Advisory Council, in recognition of services marketed to a wider clientele. The organisation publishes and markets materials for educators and other interested parties, organises training and conferences, and provides consultancy services. It has overseas contacts for information and consultancy exchange, and it will be one body to benefit greatly from an increased commitment to prevention.

## Health is Born Again

In one of those classic gaffes in the face of authoritative advice to the contrary, Government then decided to mark its widening of the DEC brief by renaming them all HEC - Health Education Co-ordinator, and making unfocused remarks as to HEC being in future responsible for health education in general. This had a number of confusing effects; not least because some schools already had teachers who were titled Health Education Co-ordinators; moreover the District Health Authorities had Health Education Units who had also been habituees of schools, albeit concentrating in the main on alcohol and tobacco. The downstream effect of all this was that some HECs lost their jobs and were replaced with new staff, many of whom were excellent teachers but had no experience relevant to illegal drugs. In other cases there were border disputes between Health (Drug) Education Co-ordinators and Health Education workers. The nett effect was and still is a dilution of drug prevention work in schools, hardly what Government could have had in mind.

The H(D)ECs are setting about rectifying this by establishing internal training and forums within their national and regional network, to share and increase knowledge. It is to be earnestly hoped that this diligence is not rendered redundant in Spring 1993, when the present funding runs out. Every indication is that when the borders in Europe come down in 1992 there will be increased passage of drugs from "stockpile countries" such as Spain. The raison d'être for DECs, even if an H(D)EC hat has to be worn, will surely strengthen for some years yet.

## Specific Initiatives in Britain and Eire

In Chapter 1 brief mention was made of four projects currently running, one in each of England, Wales, Scotland and Eire. These are indeed all "flagship" projects, but despite the excellence of each they are sailing largely alone; few other ships are as yet on the slipway, still less in the water.

## England - TEENEX

This project was designed and initiated after much self-funded and self-resourced research through literature and on project sites, by a researcher who was also a DEC (and later HEC) with a West London Borough. The programme was piloted in this borough but has also been adopted abroad, most notably in Portugal. The aim is to empower drug-free youth to stay drug-free to rely on "self, not substance", and through **informal** interchange (preaching is definitely **not** called for) and peer education methods, to encourage their peers to sustain or achieve the same lifestyle. Activities are out of school/office hours (mainly) and relate to 14-25 year olds, though the majority of participants are in the 14-19 age range. All staff are part-time volunteers. In this, Teenex differs from the Scottish, Welsh and Irish projects which generally utilise older youth as facilitators,

and have full time staff.

The project concept encompasses knowledge-giving, attitudinal and behavioural influence with a strong emphasis on peer education, through two types of initiative:

> A week-long residential camp which is carefully designed to provide an experiential process (rather than just an arbitrary collection of activities).
>
> A year-round aggregation of activities; some educational, some social, some community-based, all intended to preface and/or reinforce the effects of the Teenex camp, and disseminate these effects.

The project takes on board the reasons why young people may elect to start or continue using drugs, and explicitly addresses these (see Chapter 6). But the greater emphasis is on promoting the positives in life, not being content with the neutral state of health, that is neither ill nor well. The various constituents of health are as defined in Chapter 6: (physical/mental/emotional/spiritual/social/environmental). The project operates within specific lifestyle objectives:

> No abuse of drugs, meaning no use of any illegal substance or no misuse of any legal substance.
>
> "Misuse of legal substances" is taken to include discouragement of smoking and drinking. No alcohol is allowed on the campsite. In past years there have been strong limits on times and locations for smoking; this is likely to tighten rather than loosen, in line with current societal attitudes.
>
> Use of legal substances. Camp dwellers check their prescribed medicines into the office for safe keeping and issue as needed.
>
> A strong line against cannabis. Appendix B gives ample reason for taking this stance.
>
> Promotion of Drug-Free life (meaning drug-abuse free, see first point above).

Empowerment of young people to achieve their own effective, healthful and fulfilling lifestyle is at the core of Teenex. However, unlike some earlier programmes or policies, empowerment of youth does not mean total disempowerment of adults - parents, teachers, etc. Partnership is the aim, but a real one, in the sensible middle ground between the extremes of "leaving the kids to it" and "letting them decide the unimportant bits".

## The TEENEX Camp

This focal point to the programme has so far (in England rather than Portugal) taken place during school summer holidays so that school premises can be used. A group of around 40 youths and 10 facilitators/catering staff live on the site from Sunday afternoon to Friday night inclusive. The great majority of the youths are drug-free; a small minority may be experimenters, or ex-users or in some other way "at risk" but not more than one per small group is prudent. No one leaves except for a meal excursion on Thursday night (optional but recommended "relief" activity). The youths are merged into families (Tribes - see Chapter 4) of about 7 to 9, including a youth facilitator and an adult who takes a background role. The youth facilitators are graduates of previous programmes and they, with the adult facilitators have also received additional training prior to the camp. Some activities are conducted with the whole camp together; many are in Small Group. The Small Groups operate to the same behaviour norms as for Tribes. The youth facilitators are expected to take the lead, only involving the adult when help or guidance is called for. Strong bonding and trust develops in these small groups, where issues until now often suppressed are brought out and resolved.

A sample of the week's programme is shown in Figure 5.1. Because this is a process, not just a collection of activities, it should be conserved without structural alteration. In this context, it is noteworthy that Projecto Vida, Portugal reports that after 21 successful camps "Despite differences in our cultures we have not needed to make any changes to the programme. We find it successful every time and would recommend it to anyone". Activities are sequenced to reflect the growth of trust/openness as the days pass. They are also juxtaposed to a process rationale as follows:

| | | |
|---|---|---|
| Day 1 (evening - only) | | Registration<br>Ice-breakers |
| Day 2 | - | Getting to Know You<br>Esteem Building<br>Basic Drug Awareness |
| Day 3 | - | Extended drug information<br>Actions and Consequences<br>Teamwork |
| Day 4 | - | Self-awareness<br>Decision-making |
| Day 5 | - | Relationships<br>Sexuality |
| Day 6 | - | The future of Teenex<br>Celebrating week's achievement |

| | | | | | | | | | |
|---|---|---|---|---|---|---|---|---|---|
| MONDAY Getting to know you Esteem - building Basic drug Awareness | Welcome ! Intro. staff Rules Groups Rooms Big Hall | Getting to know you Group Rules Big Hall | Large Group Warm Fuzzies Story Big Hall | Small Groups Discuss Fuzzies Story | Large Group IALAC Big Hall | Small Groups IALAC Discussion | Large Groups Drugs – TRUE or FALSE | Small Groups TACADE card game drugs/ alco | Small Groups The Ungame |
| TUESDAY Drugs Info. Consequences Teamwork | PRIDE rehearsal Big Hall | Small Groups TACADE card games | DECISIONS Small Groups | DESERT ISLAND EXERCISES BIG HALL | | PRIDE rehearsal Big Hall | Teamwork "Business Exercise" 4:00 – 6:00 pm Big Hall | | Small Group Session |
| WEDS 'DAY Self – Awareness Decision Making | PRIDE rehearsal Big Hall | Peer Pressure Reversal Big Hall | TEAM GAME Big Hall | | Fun & Games | Skit rehearsal Small Groups | Dr. Gilkeson video on cannabis harm | Decision making | Small Groups The Ungame |
| THURSDAY Relationships | PRIDE rehearsal Big Hall | Peer Pressure Reversal Big Hall | Everything you want to know about the opposite sex.... Big Hall; Male/ female split Qs; Male/ female split As; Swop Qs As | | Young People and Sexuality Big Hall | | Small Groups Discuss Previous Session | Skit Rehearsal Small Groups | Small Group Session |
| FRIDAY The Future | PRIDE rehearsal Hogarth Stage | Small Groups Future of WYAD / TEENEX What can we do ? | ASSERTIVENESS Big Hall | | Young People And HIV / AIDS Big Hall | | Packing and Clear Site | "Pass the Paper for Strokes " Small Groups | Skits show Certificate Presentation |

**Figure 5.1 TEENEX Residential Week Programme**

Specific subjects addressed include:

- Drug/alcohol facts/mythology
- HIV/AIDS facts/mythology
- Sexuality
- Decision-making
- Assertiveness
- Peer pressure reversal
- Peer selection
- Self-esteem/Self-confidence
- Awareness of self and others
- Communications
- Goal setting, achievement, evaluation
- Groupwork
- Stress management
- Consumer skills
- Reasons for/alternatives to drug use
- Fun without drugs
- Social intercourse
- Peer counselling/co-counselling
- Peer teaching
- Group "family" feeling.

Each day is deliberately long and packed with activities. Wake-up is 0700 and work continues until 2100. Staff work on after this hour with daily review. For any youths (or adults) who have found issues raised in group sessions that they cannot handle, additional on-site counselling is available. (This could be handled by off-site counsellors on demand if your Teenex staff are not themselves trained counsellors.)

Throughout the week everyone, adults and youths, is working on songs, dances, skits to present at a Friday evening show timed to "ensnare" parents arriving to collect their charges. These presentations are helped by backing tracks supplied by the PRIDE organisation. In subsequent presentations to PTAs or school groups these "numbers" can be very effective.

Teenex has made it on to the national TV channels three times in four years, but probably more effective has been extensive and sustained local press coverage. A 100-page training pack including an 11-minute video has been produced using "home" resources and sold at cost without author's royalty. With no promotion other than a cheap photocopied flyer, every copy of the first edition has been sold, including to around one in four Local Education or Health Authorities in England.

Several overseas countries have purchased packs and some, like Panama and the New York Police Department, are known to be using it. Four other countries: Poland, Hungary, Germany and Belgium are currently seeking authorisation for Teenex trainings. In the case of Portugal, the adoption has been comprehensive. Following training of youthworkers in Lisbon by the Teenex author, Projecto Vida has run 21 camps in less than two years, training 1050 youths. These youths are now working in regional activities and also want to form a European association of drug-free youth.

## Activities other than the Camp - Peer Teaching

These have to be realistically scheduled around other demands on adolescents' time - studies, jobs, romances, sports, socialising, family life, etc. Peer teaching has been one option taken up enthusiastically; either in the form of classroom/year group presentations by Teenex graduates or in a more structured approach using proven prevention classroom activities.

Other than this, meetings open to all Teenex members, pre- or post-camp, are a mix of social and prevention activities. Visits are arranged to relevant sites such as rehabilitation units, conferences, etc. Presentations to school governors and parents can be very impactful.

A group of nine Teenex youth attended the PRIDE 91 conference in Nashville, Tennessee and made a presentation to international youth.

A very recent development has been the signing of a co-operation agreement between the Teenex author and Projecto Vida and Spain, to produce a modified version of Teenex called "Bussola" (meaning "compass", a giver of direction) for young people in care or otherwise at risk.

## Scotland - Fast Forward

Starting from "concern over a heroin epidemic in the mid 80s", Fast Forward rapidly learnt that the drug use arena in which youth circulates is much more complex than that. To keep up with a fast-changing scene and to evolve strategies with which youth would identify, Fast Forward rooted itself "firmly on the side of young people". Rooting is one thing; growth is another, but in this case healthy growth followed. As their 1990 report says, "When Fast Forward began three years ago, it had no idea that young people would play such a central role in the project's development. That they have is both to its credit and its advantage". Born at the end of 1986 out of a joint funding application by the Scottish Association of Youth Clubs and the Scottish Health Education Group, the seminal stage in late 1985 included the Director of the Scottish Association of Youth Clubs visiting the USA to observe youth drug prevention programmes.

A full time co-ordinator was appointed in April 1987 and is still with the project. He now has a development worker and a project worker to assist. One of the co-ordinator's first tasks was to explore the youth work scene; how did it tackle drug issues in general and prevention in particular? Another was to explore the scope for prevention work by local drugs agencies. The answer to both these enquiries was largely negative; youth workers tended to regard drug use as something to deal with on an individual basis once it had happened, and drug agencies were in the main too overloaded with crisis intervention to have time for prevention. If nothing else, this gave Fast Forward a clear field.

Work started in and around the capital, Edinburgh, and used a dialogue approach to draw out the "client" group's views on the subject. From this market survey pilot visits were made to clubs, working with 12 to 18 club members for one and a half to two hours. Ideas were tried and retained or ditched. A workshop format emerged of team introduction/ice breakers/discussion prompts such as quizzes, questionnaires, role-plays and competitions/synthesis into an agreed group statement about the issue. Three hallmarks were "listen, inform, challenge". Always starting by listening.

It soon became clear that talking about drugs on their own was potentially counterproductive; placing the topic within ongoing discussion of health-related issues made more sense. There also needed to be extensive attention to legal drugs - alcohol, tobacco, solvents which were more relevant to most young people.

From this low-profile beginning Fast Forward moved into a wide variety of new areas. Arts and the media were involved. Murals were produced in Edinburgh and Glasgow. Videos of workshop sessions have been used to encourage other clubs to make their own videos. A collage depicting a girl's attitudes to drugs was produced across the Lothian region. "Sam Smoke" a 15-foot high puppet made his impressive entrance in a 1989 anti-smoking campaign. Raps have been produced by youth club members. Probably the most significant arts initiative is the play "Thunderbirds and Snakebites", produced jointly with Catch, an Edinburgh-based women's theatre company. The play focuses on young women and alcohol, and was targeted at 12-16 year olds. Audience participation was actively sought, and audiences had to vote on which of two endings they required. Performances were in front of deliberately small all-girl audiences in youth clubs and the 45-minute play was followed by 45 minutes of discussion. An extensive tour of Scotland was constantly unable to fulfil all the demands for appearances, so a professional video package costing £20,000 was produced to allow others to benefit from the show-and-discussion format.

Another development came from pressure by youth workers in the more distant reaches of Scotland. How could such outposts receive more than a flying visit? The answer was the Fast Forward Roadshow, touring with three of the project's full time staff and three volunteers. But rather than just drive in/drive out, the visits were preceded (and followed) by workshops in clubs in the area. Radio and TV gave good coverage of each area visit. In some cases, "Thunderbirds and Snakebites" was also staged to coincide with the project team visit. Leader training also helped empower local workers.

More recently, Fast Forward has become further involved in peer group education. This has required a greater autonomy for young volunteer workers and, of course, a larger number of them. The former telephone networking system has been replaced by "SMUT" a fanzine for the organisation. As well as the videos mentioned above, Fast Forward also markets a training pack which has been well received by youth workers. Formal evaluations are in progress by the University of Strathclyde on behalf of the Scottish Education Department, and by Touche Ross Management Consultants on behalf of the Scottish Home and Health Department. Meanwhile, development consultants have been retained to plan the future.

## Eire - Youth to Youth

Prevention initiatives in England (Teenex), Scotland (Fast Forward) and Wales (Youthlink) have all benefited from first-hand observation of relevant work in America. No direct link between Youth to Youth and USA projects is known of, but there was definite and sustained contact between Dublin (the birthplace and base of Youth to Youth) and America. Mrs Grainne Kenny, for many years with the Community Drugs Project in Dublin and now in private practice, is an internationally-accredited authority on community drugs prevention. Grainne has maintained links with PRIDE in the USA.

Youth to Youth (Y2Y) is the brainchild of the Catholic Social Service Conference (CSSC). The CSSC was founded in 1941 to serve many aspects of the social scene in the Dublin Diocese. In 1984 CSSC launched its Drug Awareness Programme as "a response to the problems caused by drugs". The programme has an Adult and a Youth component. Although drug problems were the spur and the programme does offer counselling and referral services, "its main focus is on prevention of drug and alcohol-related problems".

Growing out of this global programme, the Y2Y scheme is co-ordinated by full time staff but makes very high use of volunteers. In particular, unemployed youths in their early 20s are given a year's paid employment under "a kind of YTS scheme" to work with Y2Y. This has the plus of attracting recruits but the frustration of losing them again just when they are getting somewhere.

These youths travel in teams of four, visiting schools, drop-in centres, youth clubs, youth training centres and other locations. They have been trained in how to produce and stage role-plays, using humour as well as facts to pose questions for later group discussion by the audience. Videos, slideshows and questionnaires can also be used to provoke dialogue.

The youth presenters "teach young people four things:

- Why to say No to Drugs
- How to say No to Drugs
- How to Enjoy Drug-Free Activities
- How to Support Each Other in Remaining Drug-Free"

The programme is adaptable to any age group from 11 upwards. It purposely avoids creating a mystique around drugs. It places high importance on the value of family, and as might be expected from a religious-based organisation, it does not shrink from defining behavioural boundaries on the basis of moral standards.

The teams offer a range of visit programmes, from a single 70 to 85-minute session up to four 35 to 45-minute sessions. They will also assist in organising specific projects, parents' sessions and the like. Wherever possible, two of the team will visit beforehand to meet the class informally, at breaks. The role-plays can be very demanding; for this reason Y2Y limit their daily team workload to 2 x 80-minute sessions or 3 x 40-minute sessions.

A more recent venture has been to offer groups a "Drug-Free Adventure", outward-bound style courses for teachers and parents.

Y2Y has developed a high reputation for its work in many quarters. Probably the most striking (no pun intended) endorsement of this is the massive donation of £50,000 by international soccer star Liam Brady. This largesse allowed Y2Y to produce a video which was marketed by Warner Home Video. As the makers say "This is not a video about drugs; it is about how to avoid them". Short dramas using Y2Y members are intercut with specially commissioned rap sequences, featuring pop-video-quality editing and computer graphics. Titled "You're only going nowhere if you can't say no", the action uses the current street language of Dublin youth to inform and challenge the viewer.

**Wales - Youthlink**

In March 1985, Dr Morfydd Keen, an Associate Specialist with South Glamorgan Health Authority, embarked on a one-month study of the USA's community drug prevention programmes under the auspices of the State Department. Projects were seen in Miami, Sacramento, Kansas and New York, following a kick-off briefing in Washington DC. Another important stopover was in Atlanta, Georgia to experience the PRIDE International Conference. Dr Keen was most encouraged by the "time and energy spent by parents and drug-free young people on involving themselves in preventative measures".

Dr Keen's feedback from her tour was

a valuable input to planning drug prevention measures, but was hardly the first chapter in the story. It was in 1982 that the Working Party of the Youth Forum on Alcohol and Drugs started planning a major event. Targeting 1985 (International Youth Year), the Working Party (which is under the umbrella of the Council for Wales of Voluntary Services and was founded in 1979) set its sights on an international forum. The forum took place in July 1985 in Cardiff, and the Welsh hosted visitors from Australia, Sweden, New Zealand, Canada, USA, France, Spain, Poland, Holland, Finland, Switzerland, Norway, Morocco and England. Over 130 young people attended the four day function, which featured as its main speaker Rick Little, charismatic Founder/President of the Quest Organization in America (founded 1975) best known in this country for its Skills for Adolescence programme marketed by TACADE. Rick travelled courtesy of Lions Club International, who have also funded the equipping of British schools with Skills for Adolescence. Rick and other speakers whipped up a powerful enthusiasm for the business of drug prevention, and from the many propositions put to concluding plenaries arguably the most significant was to form a new youth drug prevention organisation - Youthlink.

Workshops subsequent to the conference selected the name Youthlink, a logo, and aims e.g. awareness-raising amongst youth; youth involved in discussion of issues; linking the youth of Wales to produce a concerted voice; recognition from public and statutory authorities; innovation in appraising the problems of youth; encouragement of responsibility by giving responsibility to youth, and co-operation with like-minded statutory and voluntary organisations.

Youthlink has lived up to these aims; it has vigorous chapters operating in many areas of Wales and pursuing a richly-varied agenda; anything from sponsored head-shaving up to and including another international conference. The latter was a "home international" - Wales, Scotland, England and Eire and was targeted at a largely adult audience: educators, youth workers, drug workers. It attracted an audience of almost 100 and featured the Youthlink, Youth to Youth, Fast Forward and Teenex programmes.

Other Youthlink activities have included peer training weekends, photographic and poster competitions, involvement with Drinkwise events, running non-alcohol bars, carnival floats, and a "Poolathon" - emptying by hand an entire swimming pool (180,000 gallons) with an hour to spare on the 24 hour target - this raised money for Telethon.

### Reflections on the Four

Comparing the above four projects from Britain and Eire, the first observation is that each is very different; the logical extension of this is that each country could benefit from having all four projects operating within its borders.

The second observation is that though all are dedicated to and do actually practise empowerment and involvement of youth, all four projects rely on adults to hold the programme together and provide the necessary professional expertise. Thirdly, three of the projects are backed by substantial organisations and have full-time staff. The fourth, Teenex, is an independent registered charity with voluntary workers; as such it is hampered in growing relative to the other projects, but is now addressing this.

Finally, although the projects are diverse they are united in their view that primary prevention of drug abuse through the promotion of a drug-free life in the context of whole health is the right and sensible strategy.

## WHY MIGHT PEOPLE USE A DRUG?

Drug use has been positively correlated* with:

* NB: Correlations are not causal!

- Knowledge of drugs
- Attitude towards use
- Intentions to use
- Use of other drugs
- Impulsive behaviour
- Alienation
- Excessive personal stress
- Sensation seeking
- Boredom
- Assertiveness
- Anti-social tendencies
- Rejection
- Reliance on peer group for information
- Scepticism about school drug education
- Scepticism about media prevention efforts
- Peer approval of deviant behaviour
- Peer pro-drug attitudes and behaviour
- Parental use of drugs and/or alcohol
- Parental medication use
- Lack of parental concern
- Parental permissiveness
- Childhood stress and trauma
- Absence of a parent
- Family instability and disorganisation
- Quality of the relationship in the family
- Over and under-evaluation by parents
- Harsh physical punishment
- Rejection by parents
- Sexual abuse when young

Source: Bill Rice, 1988

**Figure 6.1(Part 1) Correlates with Drug Use**

## WHY MIGHT PEOPLE CHOOSE NOT TO USE?

Drug use has been **negatively** correlated* with:

- Self esteem
- Liking school
- Achievement
- Decision-making
- Self-reliance
- Feelings of belonging
- Religious beliefs
- Optimism about the future
- Humanistic environment in the school
- Alternative education programmes for 'problem' young people
- Involvement of the community
- Clear, consistent child-rearing practices
- Parent religiosity
- Parental intolerance of deviance
- Preference of controls and regulations in the home
- Extended family

* NB: Correlations are not causal!
Source: Bill Rice, 1988

**Figure 6.1(Part 2) Correlates with Drug Abstinence**

# CHAPTER 6

# BRINGING IT ALL TOGETHER

Lofquist has said that prevention, to reach its full potential, must go beyond mere response to symptoms. (This is developed later in this chapter.) As a broad strategy this is impeccable, but some knowledge of what may cause societally-unacceptable behaviours is necessary to the design of positive prevention. Validating Lofquist, what prevents drug abuse may indeed also serve to prevent delinquency and socially aberrant behaviour, as was discovered by the author during an extended period acting concurrently as a Social Work Practice Teacher, consultant to Crime Concern, and Prevention Worker (in between intervention and counselling for drug and alcohol users); the technology for all three arenas showed a very substantial overlap. However, the overlap is not total; this in turn validates (if any validation were needed) the global review of prevention programmes by Bonnie Benard detailed later in this chapter. Bonnie found that for a programme to be most effective it had to specifically address drug abuse at some point.

Combining Lofquist and Benard, the recommendation is for a societal strategy which promotes a positive drug-free lifestyle. This is nothing less than a fundamental change in society ... nobody said it would be easy ...

Let us start then with some propositions as to why people may use drugs. For some the reason will be simply "I fancied it"; for others it will be buried, perhaps irretrievably, within a complex of social, familial, sexual, economic, structural and psychological factors. What is probably a universal truth is that the reason for starting is not the reason for continuing.

There are many classic texts on antecedents to drug use; Johnson, Jessor and Jessor, Kandel, Botvin, Bandura, Glenn and others give the academic foundation to prevention philosophy. Other studies collate empirical observations of drug users or non-users, correlating other observed factors derived from detailed interviews. The listings given in Figure 6.1 were derived from Canadian research (Addiction Research Foundation) provided by Bill Rice, former Executive Officer of TACADE, The Advisory Council for Alcohol and Drug Education now based in Manchester. For a large part of his 30 years in drug work in every arena, Bill has been actively espousing the cause of positive prevention, having been instrumental in the provision of the Skills for Adolesence programme, the "Minder-Double Take" video pack and the "Drug Wise" pack.

As any academic will tell you, in the context of Figure 6.1, "Correlations are Not Causal", nevertheless they do give some very useful clues to the intelligent analyst. And not all of those "positively correlating with" (i.e. perhaps causing) drug use could be termed deficit models. For example, assertiveness has been noted in some drug users ... this hardly suggests that teaching assertiveness will cause drug abuse! Most of the positive and negative correlations are more readily understandable than this.

Although Bill's lists are extensive, one could conceive of them being extended still further. However, to understand in one medium-sized nutshell what may prompt and then sustain drug use, the following model is offered. Many authorities on the subject of drug abuse boil down the reasons for abuse to just five. (A sixth reason, the Ben Johnson go-faster factor, does not apply to everyone, but the five basic reasons do). This author has suggested how these five reasons might interrelate, in a progression from "drug-free" onwards to "problem drug use", as shown in Figure 6.2.

For a hypothetical case, use starts because of curiosity, or peer pressure, or both. Having satisfied curiosity but not enjoyed it, the user may give up. Similarly, having shown peer pressurisers that the new user is "one of the gang" the user may give up, not having enjoyed it, and peers may press less in future (or may not). This phase may relate to more than one episode of use.

If however the starting user did encounter pleasure there is more likelihood of use being repeated. (Hence the outer loop on this sector.) A user could also give up at this juncture, if something or someone more pleasurable comes along. This behaviour has also been observed to be self-reinforcing, in that as a user becomes more involved in drugs as a source of pleasure, other pleasures pall and drug use becomes the automatic solution to the "Feel Good Now" quest. One of many examples is sex; some drugs reduce libido. Should a user become locked in this inner loop they may find themselves becoming problem users and even dependants. The author is currently dealing with such clients, deriving from the Rave (nee House) scene, and the use of E or Acid.

Some users find at an early stage of their drug-using "career" (another euphemism from the pro-drug lobby) that in addition to pleasure they also experience escape from life pressures, or from boredom, or both. The preliminary likely consequence of this is that use will be repeated for either or both these reasons. (Hence the outer loops again on these sectors.) In each case however there is the potential for self-reinforcement. In the case of boredom, some drugs such as heroin and cannabis can make a person more demotivated and therefore more bored when not stoned. In the case of escape, it is likely that if a person's new(ish) drug use is discovered by others that pressure (hassle) on them will increase, i.e. there is more to escape from. Escape from potential withdrawal is another motivation. The downstream result of these reinforced behaviours is likely to be problematic use, and perhaps dependency. Once again, there is the possibility of giving up, especially if there are large changes in life (like finding a deep relationship or going to prison). As with quicksand, the further in you get, the tougher it is to get out.

For the record, Peer Pressure is the reason most youth start abuse while Escape is the most frequent reason for adults to abuse. This model

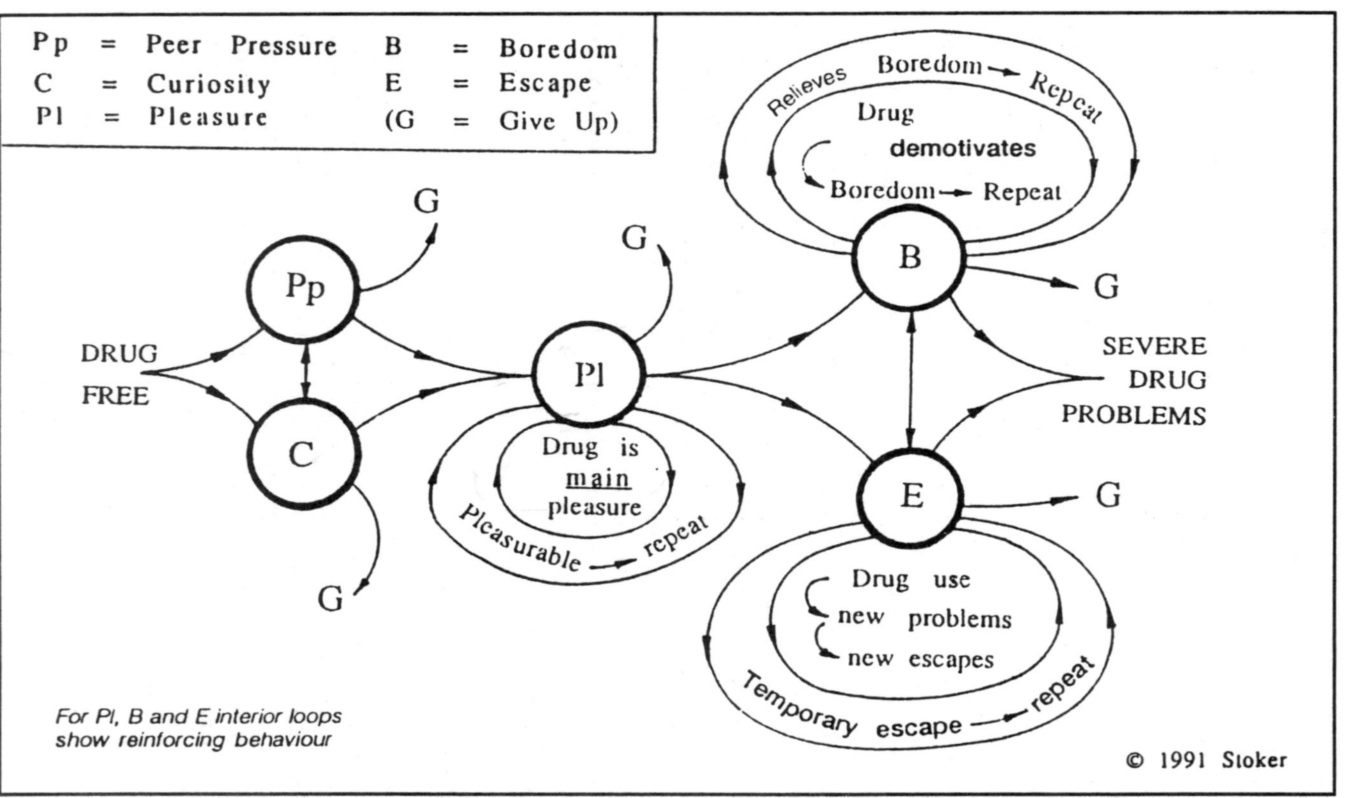


**Figure 6.2 Principle Impulses to Drug Use**

does not explicitly address structural factors such as employment, housing, environment, but the effect of these factors on the individual (positive or negative) is implicit in the model.

One question sometimes asked is where do tranquilliser dependants fit in? (Some of these have been put on tranquillisers as young as mid-teens, and dependency starts surreptitiously within three or four months). The first answer is that they did not choose to use a drug which, when starting, they knew might cause dependency; they were prescribed it and took it in good faith. Some of the reasons they used (other than muscle relaxation), particularly escape from anxiety and other stresses are similar to other drugs and thus the counselling, reduction to abstinence, and recovery stages utilise many of the therapeutic elements common to any drug problem. Once dependent they are in some cases continuing to take the drug to avoid withdrawal symptoms, as with any other dependent, but almost all are desperate to stop.

One structure of prevention could start with the model shown in Figure 6.2 and offer pre-emptive strategies for each of the five reasons. For example, expunge Curiosity by fully informing people. Risk-taking, a rite of passage with adolescents, may be seen as a combination of Curiosity/Pleasure/Escape; the strategy is to find risks that have safety nets. Peer Pressure is best dealt with by peer selection and/or peer pressure reversal techniques. The Search for Pleasure can be guided into many avenues other than drug abuse, as can the avoidance of Boredom. There is no permanent way round the Escape zone, you have to go through it, learn how to face issues and either succeed, or cope with failure. This is where structural factors come in mainly, although they also impinge on Boredom and Pleasure. Beyond this response-oriented strategy, then, what of Positive Prevention?

## The Real Prevention

The overlap in technologies between drug prevention, delinquency prevention, and behavioural modification within the Social Services context (as described at the beginning of this chapter) was an exciting discovery for this author. However, rather like being the second into the bathtub after Archimedes, it was found to be not a new discovery. In 1983 Bill W. Lofquist in the foreword to his classic book, had made the following key statement:

> "We have organised human symptoms, building entire systems that work in relative isolation from one another. Juvenile and criminal justice, education, health, public welfare, recreation and many other services function in separate spheres and there is often isolation of components even within these systems.
>
> Prevention is another matter. When I have told people I have been working on a book about prevention, the immediate question has

> often been prevention of **what**? That is a logical question in a symptom-focused, remedial, reactive world. I have purposefully left any mention of symptoms out of the title of the book. One reason is the awareness that a wide variety of symptoms are the result of some common conditions. Designing separate systems for remedial work may make some sense, but addressing the common conditions which promote those systems calls for a different approach. If we can get beyond the notion that prevention is only "stopping something from happening" to a more positive approach that creates conditions which promote the well-being of people, we can begin to view human services quite differently. This, in turn, can transform and enrich our approaches to helping people and building communities that are relatively free of the symptoms we have designed the services around".

The wider significance and potential of this finding is enormous. It means that if we can only produce and effect truly comprehensive prevention strategies there is the promise of society empowering itself to achieve improvements across a broad spectrum. Nothing solves everything, of course, and like many a good strategy it is likely to fall foul of such factors as professional and/or parochial jealousies, myopic policies, etc. Prevention workers are therefore unlikely to need to plan a fresh career for some time to come.

**Health - What is it?**

Most people today are in accord that drug prevention (or as they too-narrowly define it, drug education) is best approached as part of a broad health promotion (or ditto ditto) strategy. It is therefore useful to consider what we mean by Health.

An excellent definition was produced not a few years ago, around 1000 BC, by the Ancient Greeks, as follows:

> Wellness in physical/mental/emotional/spiritual aspects
> An active part in community life
> At one with one's environment

Wellness indicates not merely the neutral state of being "neither ill nor well" but a condition significantly above this. From this definition of the full potential a human being has, it follows that the price of drug abuse which diminishes that potential is more than anyone should in all common sense be prepared to pay.

So, we have defined why people might abuse drugs, how to not only respond to these reasons but go beyond them into positive prevention, and we have defined why we are doing this - the goal of comprehensive Health. How then can we design our prevention strategy and techniques to maximise the beneficial effect we facilitate?

## Characteristics of Effective Prevention

Given all that has been said so far about the complexity of this subject it might be thought that characteristics of effective strategies (or sections thereof) might be as elusive as angel feathers. Certainly the "school of prevention" could benefit from much more academically rigorous evaluation of what is being done worldwide, and funders should take this need for evaluation into account when sizing grants.

Nevertheless, there have been several excellent research initiatives, for example the monograph "Prevention Research Findings, 1988" (printed 1990), produced by the (American) Office of Substance Abuse Prevention (OSAP). OSAP set out to compress the timescale between observation of fieldwork and publication of research, and to bring hands-on workers closer to researchers. They did this through mounting a First National Conference on Prevention Research Findings. OSAP assembled "twenty exemplary community prevention programs", together with prevention researchers, policy makers, and service providers. The proceedings of that conference went into this monograph. It is required reading for any prevention worker.

Meanwhile, as you wait for your copy of the OSAP monograph to arrive from Washington DC, the following checklist is an invaluable foundation to the design of any prevention strategy. It is the brainchild of Bonnie Benard, currently with the afore-mentioned OSAP, and acknowledged as one of the gurus of prevention research.

The following section is largely an abbreviated version of Bonnie's listing, itself derived from a combination of literature review and comparison (Benard, 1987). Certain sections have been modified or augmented to take account of research and application by others including the author, or to relate better to the British situation. The recommendations come under three broad headings of programme comprehensiveness/intensity; programme strategies; and lastly programme planning.

## Programme Comprehensiveness/Intensity

A. **Multiplicity:** the causes of drug/alcohol abuse are multiple: personality, environmental, behavioural (Kandel, Logan, 1984; Hawkins et al, 1985). Programmes tackling only one area usually fail. You should target multiple systems (youth, families, schools, community, workplace, media, etc). Also use multiple strategies (information, lifestyles, positive alternatives, community policies) (Botvin, 1982).

B. **Target whole community**. School-based programmes benefit less than community-based approaches.

C. **Target all youth**, not just "high risk". Adolescence is seen to be a high-risk time for all youth in terms of health-compromising behaviour. Labelling "high-risk" youth can provoke stigmatisation and thence self-fulfilling prophecies. There is however an argument for defining 'high-risk' communities where an additional resource over and above the general prevention effort could be justified.

D. **Build drug prevention into general health promotion**. Drug abuse has been found by several (Lofquist, 1983) to interrelate, to be part of a constellation of interconnected factors - delinquency, truancy, school failure, precocious sexuality, which share common antecedents.

E. **Start early and keep going!** Even in infancy there are influences in later behaviour. Developmental difficulties by age 3 are difficult to overcome (Burton White).

Here it is of course relevant to mention Trefor Williams, Noreen Wetton and Alysoun Moon of the Southampton University team who have demonstrated so graphically in their "Jugs and Herrings" research paper that primary age children are not blissfully ignorant of drugs and alcohol. Prevention programmes starting from what the children actually know are essential.

Many secondary schools still seem to regard Years 11 and 12 as the age at which discussion of drugs (or indeed sexuality) should be facilitated. Stable doors and horses come to mind!

F. **Adequate quantity**. "One-shot prevention efforts do not work" (Kumpfer, 1988). There must be a substantial number of interventions, each of a substantial duration.

Project DARE (Drug Abuse Resistance Education) initiated by Los Angeles Police and now in several other states delivers no less than seventeen two hour lessons to any given year - and this is only part of the school programme.

G. **Integrate** family/classroom/school/community life. This is easier to say than to do, but where it has happened results have been enhanced.

H. **Supportive environment, empowerment**. Where young people are encouraged to participate and take responsibility their behavioural outcomes are improved. In Britain now peer-teaching methods proven elsewhere are being piloted; the author's experience in this context is described earlier in this book. (See TRIBES and TEENEX Chapters 4 and 5 respectively.)

**Programme Strategies**

J. **Knowledge/Attitudes/Behaviour**. Address these as a set, i.e. each must be directly tackled rather than assuming one will flow

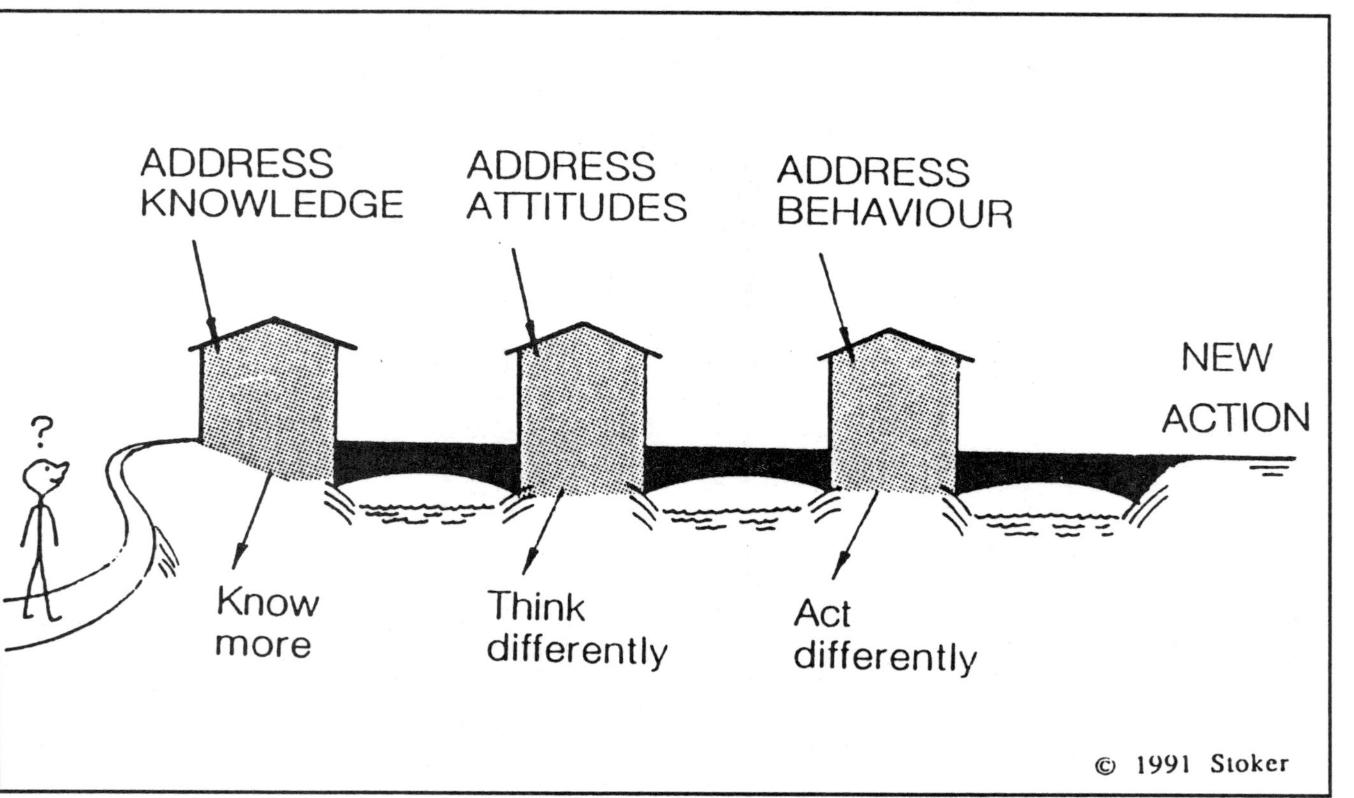


**Figure 6.3 Three Bridges to Cross**

from another. Figure 6.3 demonstrates this graphically. The behavioural component is in part addressed by social skills development, but also supported by positive reinforcement activites - drug free social/sporting events, commendations (preferably with something for everyone), media coverage, etc. Research suggests that Social Learning Theory (Bandura, 1977) produces some of the most profound improvements.

K. **Drug specific curriculum**. Affective education programmes which had not specifically covered drugs (including alcohol) were found unsuccessful, even though they addressed knowledge, attitudes and lifeskills.

L. **Gateway drugs**. So called because people now using heavy-end drugs almost always started on these. Gateway drugs are tobacco, alcohol and cannabis. Concentration on prevention of these is therefore likely to prevent all substances. British research by MORI, (Parents against Tobacco, 1990) showed that of youth who smoked tobacco 50% had also tried an illegal drug compared with only 2% of those who did not smoke tobacco. It should be particularly noted that cannabis is far from harmless; physical, mental and social damage is now being increasingly accepted by all but the most dedicated protagonists. Appendix B tells you more on this.

M. **Salient material**. Whatever is used needs to identify with the audience, including:

- Ethnic/cultural sensitivity
- Appeal to youth's interests
- Short term outcomes to be emphasised as important to youth as well as long term
- Appropriate language, readability
- Appealing graphics
- Appropriate to real age/reading age - a key factor:

In a survey of 3,700,000 young American children, 25% of 9 year olds felt "some" to "a lot" of peer pressure to try drugs or alcohol (Weekly Reader, 1987).

N. **Alternatives**. Activities have to be plausible, be more highly valued than the health-compromising behaviour. Too often these alternatives are poorly thought through.

.P. **Lifeskills**. Development of these will be of wider benefit than drug prevention. Included will be Communication, Problem-Solving, Decision-Making, Critical Thinking, Assertiveness, Peer Pressure Reversal, Peer Selection, Low-Risk Choice Making, Self Improvement, Stress Reduction and Consumer Awareness (Botvin, 1985).

Choosing your friends has been found in some research to be more effective than resisting the peer pressure of said friends. Consumer awareness is a "companion" to resisting peer pressure, i.e. resisting media pressure.

Q. **Training prevention workers**. For the school setting the greater emphasis on experimental and interactive work requires teacher training to extend into youth work skills. Community development skills are valuable in taking school initiatives into the community. Imported 'prestige' role models are all very well, but good results have been achieved with parents, peers, teachers, or outside agency workers.

R. **Community norms**. Consistency of policies throughout schools, families and communities can greatly enhance impact.

S. **Alcohol norms**. Because of its dual status as a beverage and as a culturally accepted drug, alcohol is problematic for prevention. However, heart disease and tobacco prevention programmes have shown that societal norms can be changed.

T. **Improve schooling!** Listed here as a target because of its important correlation with healthy lifestyle. Within the current British economic and academic climate the most realistic hope may lie with co-operative learning - there is more on this in Chapter 4 (see TRIBES).

U. **Change Society**. Don't just stop with improving schools; add your voices to pressure for improvement in employment, housing, recreation and self-development. It is naive to suppose that prevention can take place in a political vacuum. Jessor recognises that failing to acknowledge the need for macro-environmental improvement while at the same time placing the responsibility for health solely with the individual is tantamount to "blaming the victim".

## The Planning Process

V. **Design, implementation, evaluation**. Evaluations have generally concentrated on outcomes rather than the quality of design. However, implementation is as much dependent on engaging all sectors of the community (be it a school, a workplace, or a town) as it is on quality of design. Evaluation should therefore measure process as well as outcome.

W. **Goal-setting**. Unrealistic or immeasurable goals help no-one. It is important to set not only long-term outcome goals (for prevention is long-term) but also "process goals" such as increased involvement of parents and community, academic success, increased student-teacher interaction, and so on.

X. **Evaluation and amendment**. Prevention workers have been criticised for giving too little attention to this area; the crushing shortage of funds has much to do with it (in America the ratio of funding between interdiction-policy and prevention is about 200:1). This lack of emphasis on evaluation has been the Achilles heel which pro-drug campaigners have gleefully attacked.

> Effective evaluations have been those including longitudinal design, multiple measures of process as well as outcome (Tobler, 1986), and cost-benefit analysis (CBA). CBA is perhaps the greatest marketing tool prevention has; where CBA has been applied substantial cost- effectiveness has been demonstrated.
>
> Feedback from ongoing evaluation will, in the most effective programmes, result in rapid changes to mirror the dynamic nature of the environment.

To some it may seem that Bonnie's listing swings from the prosaic to the profound, the practical to the preposterous ... "Change Society"?! This is the time to remember Shaw's dictum on the value of the Unreasonable Man. (see Chapter 1). Moreover, taking an overview of the broad strategy empowers the field worker to see his/her place in the pattern and thus act with greater assurance. Think globally, act locally.

It should also be remembered that America has had more than fifteen years' hard-won experience in building up the level of expertise evidenced by the above schedule (and by publications such as OSAP Research Monograph 3, referred to earlier). We may be close behind in abusing drugs, but in preventing abuse we are years behind several countries, not just America.

We are famed for our Dunkirk spirit in Britain. Sometimes it seems that we have to get into a Dunkirkian situation before we produce our best. As citizens interested in primary prevention we have to recognise that Dunkirk is too late. We don't want things to reach the severe drug abuse conditions in America before we finally galvanise ourselves. We have to work hard now, campaign now, Just Say NOW.

# APPLICATION OF THE TECHNOLOGY

## WARNING SIGNS FOR WORKAHOLICS

*Often feeling wound-up and finding it hard to unwind.

*Seeing work as the most important aspect of your life, above family and friends.

*Always having work with you, thinking about work and finding it difficult to switch it off.

*Being reluctant to take time off for weekends and holidays.

*If you do take time off, phoning the office repeatedly or feeling generally ill at ease.

*Hating to delegate.

*Trying to save time by doing several work activities at once.

*Making mistakes at work because of hurrying.

*Becoming unreasonably impatient in queues or slow moving traffic.

*Using work as an excuse to avoid family or social responsibilities.

**From "Compulsion" by Robin Blake and Eleanor Stephens**

**(pub. Boxtree 1987 for Thames Television).**

**Figure 7.1 Overload Indicators**

# CHAPTER 7

# A MODEL PREVENTION STRATEGY

In his masterly book on drug prevention "Before It's Too Late" Ernst Servais of Belgium speaks repeatedly of "global" and "holistic" strategies. By "global" he means covering every component of society, and by "holistic" he means addressing every element of a person's make-up: physical, mental, emotional, spiritual. Neither in society nor in humanity is there stability, therefore any strategy has to be ready to react to (or better yet, anticipate) changes.

This concept could paralyse you if you let it. There is no need. The task of covering society breaks down into readily-definable segments, geographical/discipline-based. As to being aware of and interacting with the six elements (physical, mental, emotional, spiritual, social, environmental) of health promotion stated in Chapter 6, this is something we all do instinctively to a greater or lesser extent. The important thing is to raise our awareness of the six elements, and be sensitive to each person's needs in respect of each element, getting help in good time when it is considered necessary. In this context there is one extremely important person to consider.

## Looking After Yourself

Burn-out in the caring professional, or in those who contribute in their off-duty hours to caring activities like drug prevention, is almost a badge of pride, a battle honour to be stitched onto our personal flag. The flag is pretty tattered of course, because we never have time to fix it; other people's flags are much more important, are they not?

Well, is that true? Are you a prime burn-out candidate? Are you a workaholic? (See Figure 7.1). Are you even what drug counsellors would call "co-dependent", meaning that you subjugate your own needs, your own persona to other people in a behavioural syndrome as compulsive in its own way as that of the drug dependant or alcoholic whose image first prompted you to get into prevention work?

If you are any of these things it certainly does not mean you should shun any kind of caring work, but it does mean (to put it in drug terms) that you should consider a policy of Harm Reduction. You have elected to experience drug prevention, so make sure you use the least risky method.

One of PRIDE's most celebrated speakers is Ann Meyer, a past president of the National Federation of Parents for Drug-Free Youth. From her popular presentation entitled "Ann's Tip's for a Beautiful Burnt-Out You", Figure 7.2, gives a sampler which you can use to rate your chances of producing burn-out in yourself, or others.

## THE BURNOUT QUIZ

| | | |
|---|---|---|
| SA | Strongly Agree | =10 points |
| A | Agree | = 7 points |
| D | Disagree | = 3 points |
| SD | Strongly Disagree | = 0 points |

1. I always seem to feel fatigued throughout the day.
2. I find myself talking less and less in business and social meetings.
3. My memory seems to be deteriorating - I'm forgetting more and more.
4. Even after a good night's sleep, I still feel tired.
5. I find it very difficult to really relax - my mind always seems to in full gear thinking about work.
6. At the end of each day, I feel that I'm further behind than when I started the day.
7. I seem to be more irritable and cranky lately. I am not as patient with others. I have a short fuse and blow up easily.
8. I am spending less and less time on physical activities and hobbies or with my family and friends.
9. I seldom seem to be pleased with what I've already accomplished. I feel that I should be accomplishing more.
10. I either operate at full speed ahead or at dead asleep - no middle ground.

## SCORING

| | |
|---|---|
| 0 - 5 points | -You either don't do anything or you've really got your act together. |
| 16 - 50 points | You're doing well. At this level, you're highly unlikely to suffer from burnout. |
| 51 - 80 points | You're on thin ice and just about ready to fall in. You'd better change your lifestyle quickly because burnout is knocking down your door. |
| 86 - 100 points | I'm glad I don't work for you or with you. You are a walking time bomb. If you do not make immediate adjustments in your behaviour you may be burned out by the time you finish reading this article. |

**Source: Ann Meyer**

**Figure 7.2 : How to do Burnout**

Having equipped you to service, maintain and function to your best, let's see who else could help you.

## Everyone Can Help

The natural response in the face of drug problems in general is to regard them hopefully as someone else's problems. We ourselves are "too unskilled", "too committed in other fields", and certainly "too busy to be involved". Even if the problem seems to be coming closer to home the response is likely to be similar. It has been said that in the context of drugs the three most dangerous words are not Alcohol, Cannabis and Heroin; they are **"Not My Kid"**.

A film of this title gave a salutory story of a white middle-class family whose daughter became involved in drugs. The father, played by George Segal, went into a classic denial syndrome. The subsequent action centred around a youth rehabilitation unit very close in character to the real-life Straight Centres (a controversial programme but, from personal extended observation, very effective). It was an object lesson for us all, whether we have children of our own or not. For the real point is that we are **all** empowered through our concern and commitment, and through the efforts we put in to make ourselves aware and informed, to perform the role of parent, brother, sister, etc. in the community at large.

Prevention, then, is a matter of attitude, a state of mind. Just as orienting a whole workforce to have marketing in mind can uplift that company's fortunes, so is it with prevention. You do not have to be prevention experts anymore than you have to be marketing experts, but if you are pushing in that direction, your push with thousands of others will have a profound effect.

Surely though this does not have to engage the whole community? Won't this be an unbalanced deployment of resources? The answer to the first is that the whole community does indeed have to be involved, since we are talking of nothing less than a radical shift in the attitudes of all ages, but particularly the "intractable" young. Answering the second, resource deployment would not be unbalanced, since only limited contingents from each sector would be substantially involved - most of us would continue largely as now, but with a greater awareness of the factors, dangers and implications of drug abuse. We would also have a greater appreciation of the bonus in promise for life factors such as relationships, and for increased general effectiveness of society, accruing from a "global and holistic" prevention approach. A further retort to the resource balance question might be to point out how much is currently spent on helicoptors, launches, staff, etc. to intercept at best 10% of the drugs traffic coming through, compared to the pittance spent on prevention. Is this "balance"?

To give an example of a whole community approach (where "community" can mean your school, your company, or your town - and then all of these summated) the following passage is taken from Curriculum Guidance 5: "Health Education" produced by the National Curriculum Council:

> "Health education in schools does not begin and end in the classroom. The subtle messages that pupils receive about health from the daily life of a school are as important as those given during lessons. The message thus conveyed should be consistent... the aims, attitudes, values and procedures of a school are fundamental to the success of any health education programme."

Staying with the example of a school community for a moment, this community does not stop at the school gates. Parents are a vital part of the community, and the new procedures for LMS - Local Management of Schools -.may give an ideal fresh opportunity to involve school governors, and parents at large. Similar boundary definitions/"catchment areas" can be applied to businesses, and obviously apply to outreaching organisations such as youth clubs and churches.

Co-operation on prevention matters will bring with it bonuses in other aspects of community life as new productive acquaintanceships are cemented. It also brings certain risks. The prevention co-operative venture needs to take careful account of existing relevant bodies and not tread on their toes. Most Health Authority Districts have a DDAC - District Drugs Advisory Committee - which is responsible for co-ordinating statutory and voluntary action on drugs including alcohol. Your prevention venture has a right to sit on the DDAC. Agenda will relate to **all** aspects of drug/ alcohol use: prevalence surveys, intervention, treatment, detoxification, rehabilitation, outreach, harm reduction, advice, counselling, referrals, law and order, social matters, pharmacies, education, and (probably last) prevention, so don't expect to hold the floor for long! The DDAC will also have representatives acting on related subjects, such as HIV/AIDS groups. With the onset of the Community Care Act the responsibility for co-ordinating policy on drug and alcohol matters passed to Social Services, so that DDACs now (usually) answer to a CCPG - Community Care Planning

Group- linking Health and Social Services senior management, who hear policy and expenditure proposals from the DDAC and (hopefully) endorse and fund these proposals.

DDACs are generally acknowledged to be something of a mixed bag; they don't meet very often, and whilst some have been very purposeful, (usually where members are senior enough to take decisions in mobilising departments and to commit funds on the spot), others have been emasculated talking shops with a networking benefit but not much else. Even at this lower level of effectiveness however, they are worth attending, so that relevant community and statutory groups get to know your venture and - not least - so that you can lobby for a higher profile being given to primary prevention, higher than the 'poor cousin' position it has suffered in the past in Britain.

**Talk To Me**

From this is follows that you will need to establish your own communication and coordination network, not over-reaching yourself. Start close by and work outwards. (See also the Texans War on Drugs networking model in Figure 12.1.) Perhaps one method of starting your networking exercise would be to list everyone you think you should be "interfacing" with, then rate then from 1 to 5 for value to your project.

Where do you get your lists? Pool your mental list with that of others in your action group. If you don't have an action group, are trying to promote prevention all on your own, go back and read the pages on burn-out again.

Libraries are an excellent source of community information. You may also have some kind of voluntary action centre, an umbrella for local voluntary groups; tap into this at an early date. Churches of all varieties, youth clubs and the Youth Service are all useful contacts. The Youth Service may have a good directory. People like the Citizens Advice Bureaux, Community Associations are another source of information... help maybe. Your Local Education Authority should be able to put you onto School Governors Co-ordinators, if any. Failing this, write to schools individually - primary as well as secondary - and ask for your letter to be passed on to Governors and also to Parent Associations. You may even decide to ask for a copy to be sent to the teacher who co-ordinates Health Education in the school, at the very least this courtesy will be good PR, but you may get lucky and pick up a valuable recruit.

Another invaluable contact point for recruits is your local Volunteer Bureau. This is an employment agency for volunteers, and just like the regular Job Centre the better specification you can give as to the help you need, the more useful will be the people they send along. Help in even the most prosaic areas can be a lifesaver, and spurning such help on the grounds that you don't have time for learning curves is burnoutspeak.

## Is There a Prevention Doctor in the House?

Perhaps the first question to ask. Who is already working on drug matters in your area? Are you lucky enough to have one of the (Home Office) Local Drug Prevention Units covering your area, or near enough that you could make contact with a view to future friendly advice? What local drug agencies are there and do they do any **primary** prevention work? If not, in what way might they co-operate? Does your local hospital have a DDU (Drugs Dependency Unit) or contacts with doctors who have expertise in this field? They could be star turns when you embark on public meetings. Is there a Health Education Unit? -- Be grateful if there is, they can give you valuable advice, can dispense mega quantities of free leaflets, posters, etc. and can mount very impressive displays at the conferences or meetings you convene.

Be aware of one thing, however, with the Health Education Authority. The main thrust of their work is not, thus far, towards the illegal side of the drug abuse business. They do a great deal of valuable work on legal drugs such as tobacco and alcohol, but their latest annual report does not even mention illegal drugs. You could be one of the people to help them rectify that imbalance.

**Further Afield**

There is validity in looking to the distance for help at the same time as working locally. Just be sure you know why you're doing what you're doing, and for how long. An example might be attending a national or even international conference - often an inspirational event that will enable you to energise many others for months afterwards. If you learn of someone doing something similar to (or better than) you, having read of this in the specialised journals you now avidly consume, why not write to them and fix a visit? Don't be shy. This kind of "on-spec" interested contact got this writer into The White House Old Executive Office and specifically into the office of the President's Advisor on Substance Abuse; a valuable and informative meeting concluded with our hosts saying "Well, it was real nice of you to drop by. You're the first people to have ever done that!".

Even if you don't make actual visits, at least write and establish an information exchange. Drug abuse is a world problem but drug prevention is a world solution. **Think globally, act locally.** There are many invaluable sources of guidance out there just waiting to hear from you. And as the man said, a stranger is just a friend you haven't met yet.

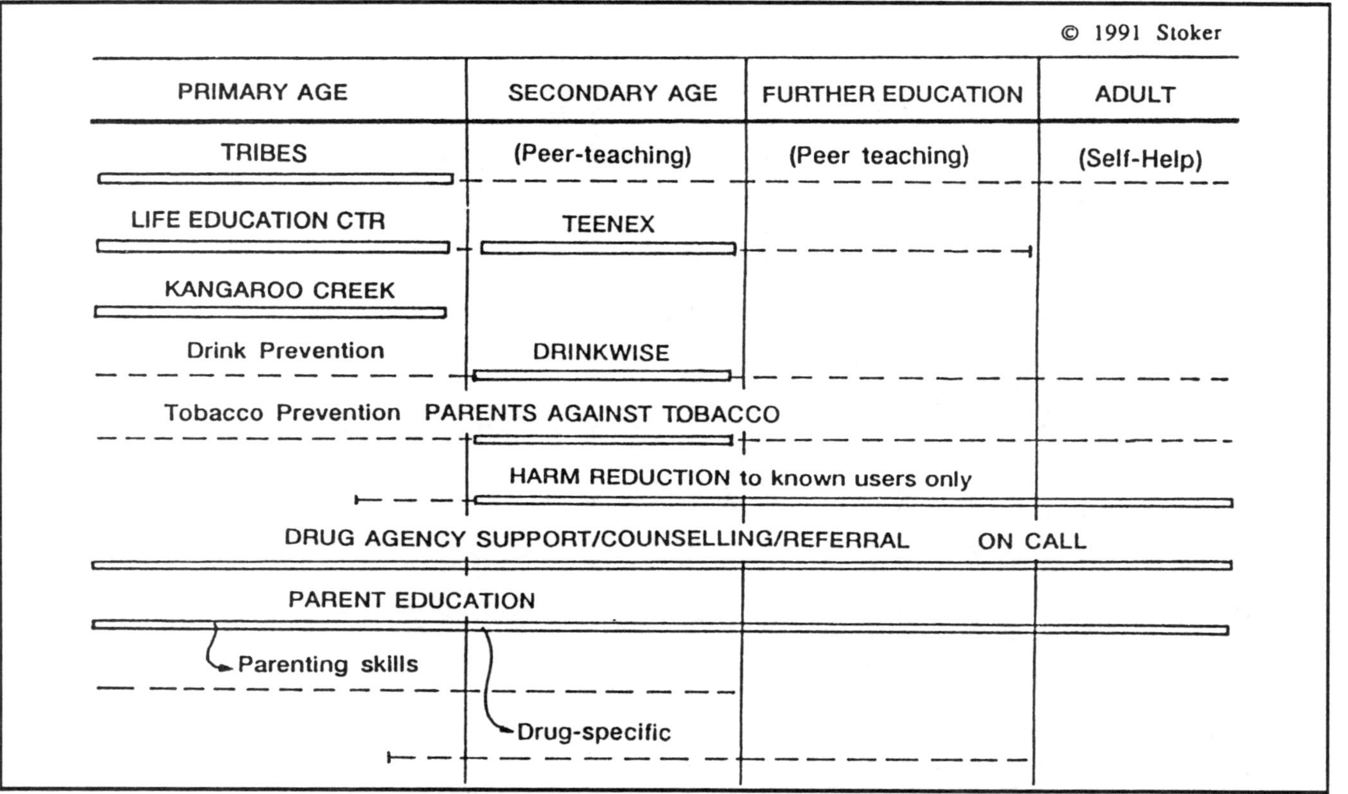


**Figure 8.1 A Contiguous Strategy for Drug Prevention**

## CHAPTER 8

# PROCESS AND PROGRAMME SPECIFICS

In the first "half" of this book the technical and philosophical basis for prevention was set out, with the criteria for effective processes. One could fill suitcases with research papers expanding on all these criteria, so maybe it would help to distil them down to three words: Long, Wide, Deep.

Long, meaning start young and keep going.
Wide, meaning involve the whole community.
Deep, meaning Knowledge + Attitudes + Behaviour.

Considering the above-described three-dimensional structure, like all structures it is stronger if there are no gaps in it, and if there are frequent cross-links. Thus, the "length", starting young, should be sustained throughout primary, secondary, further education, adulthood into old age. There should certainly be liaison between primary, secondary and further education in a given locality, to ensure a rational progression of personal development. The "width" across the community should engage every sector and encourage them to engage with each other. The "depth" should be appropriate to the age, but should over a period encompass, reiterate and reinforce (a process some call Spiral Learning) the three essential components of knowledge, attitudes and behaviour. "Cross Linkage" merely refers to integrating the length/width/depth considerations to ensure that at any position in the structure a person is able to obtain prevention assistance of appropriate duration, intensity, sophistication and relevancy to the recipient's environment.

### A Model Timetable

Figure 8.1 illustrates a specimen timetable for a contiguous prevention strategy. A number of specific programmes are listed as young people progress from primary age onwards. The programmes/processes: "Tribes", "Life Education" and "Kangaroo Creek" are all described in some detail in Chapter 4 and Teenex in Chapter 5. Tribes in particular can continue to be applied right through succeeding age groups, as it has already in practice, up to and including adults in employment.

In the adult stage Tribes (or other programmes) can also be supplemented by EAPs - Employee Assistance Programmes - the latter having a prevention value as well as their traditional justification of intervention. That is to say, by intercepting the concerns, stresses and problems of an employee early you may well help that person avoid resorting to tranquillisers, alcohol, perhaps lapsing back into smoking, or even opting for illegal drugs. There is great promise in the field of EAPs which Britain has yet to grasp, but to have a preventive value and to encourage maximum use by employees with alcohol/drug problems it must be a full EAP - see Chapter 4.

So, what else should be happening back at the time when young people are at primary age? In fact work can start sooner than this; once a child is born (or even sooner) parents can learn parenting skills, many of which can have the eventual effect of preventing various negative behaviours. Arguably, one of the greatest omissions in our schooling is the lack of any coaching in parenting skills, despite this being one of the tasks in adult life which almost all of us have to confront. This subject is enlarged on in Chapter 11.

For the primary pupils themselves, whichever programme is the core of their health education, it should explicitly include smoking prevention and alcohol **prevention, not** "sensible drinking". The strong correlation between avoidance of smoking and drinking, up to and through adolescence, and the avoidance of illegal drug use has been repeatedly proved. If schools take a firm line on promoting a smoke-free/drink-free life, starting in primary school this will pay big dividends later. Once into the secondary school environment there are specific programmes such as "Parents Against Tobacco" and "Drinkwise" to help reinforce the earlier learning, though there should certainly be regular and ongoing classroom work to act as the foundation to these activities. Chapter 9 says more on this.

Mention of Drinkwise in the context of secondary schools raises a thorny dilemma. As already said, avoidance of drink throughout adolescence strongly indicates avoidance of illegal drugs forever. Some US prevention agencies press this line very hard - see Figure 8.2. But is total abstention realistic in British culture, let alone the viniculture of Europe? Drinkwise have decided not, but from discussion with colleagues involved in the Drinkwise project it becomes clear that one factor (amongst several) is that opting for "sensible drinking" by teenagers, and younger

**WHY ADOLESCENTS SHOULD NOT USE ALCOHOL AT ALL!**

Gail Romano, PRIDE Speakers Bureau, is quite straightforward about it:
"If this sounds like a hard-line approach, it's because it is and there are reasons for it.

1.First of all adolescents get addicted more quickly than adults do because their bodies are still growing. It takes an adult five to fifteen years to become physically addicted to alcohol. IT TAKES AN ADOLESCENT SIX MONTHS TO TWO YEARS. (This growth process continues until approximately twenty-four years of age.)

2.Secondly, teenagers do not drink socially ... they drink to get high or drunk. (That statement comes from the young people themselves, folks, so I think that we adults should start to listen!). Drinking to get high or drunk is one of the early warning signs of an impending drinking problem. AND, YES, TWO BEERS WILL GET A TEENAGER HIGH.

3.Thirdly, when parents allow their teenagers to drink, the are in effect giving an "I don't care about you" message. They know that it's harmful and yet they allow their children to indulge. The end result is that the child feels unloved and uncared for.

**PARENTS ARE SUPPOSED TO SET LIMITS! THAT'S THEIR JOB.THE YOUNGSTERS EXPECT IT AND DEEP DOWN THEY WANT IT!**

4.Fourth, parents give their young people the message that they think that it's in order to break the law when they allow them to drink. In this country, young people over sixteen can buy and drink beer, cider, porter or perry (but not wine) with a meal in a restaurant. However, it is **illegal** to buy alcohol in a licensed premises or consume any intoxicating liquor in a bar under the age of eighteen.

5.Fifth and finally, because alcohol is a sedative drug, as little as one or two beers begins to put the brain to sleep. The result is that co-ordination, judgement and reflexes are impaired. When driving, that can be the difference between an accident and a near miss. When studying for an exam, that can be the difference between an A and a B.

**NOW ... DO YOU WANT YOUR TEENAGERS TO DRINK?!**
**FOR ADOLESCENTS, THERE IS NO SUCH THING AS "RESPONSIBLE USE" OF AN ILLEGAL SUBSTANCE."**

Source : PRIDE

**Figure 8.2 A Hard Line on the Hard Stuff**

even, is simply another facet of the Harm Reduction v Prevention debate. That is, some of those opting to allow "sensible drinking" (or "responsible drinking" - see "Weasel Words" later in this chapter) do so because they are ideologically opposed to prevention.

Others do so because they don't really see how they can stop it, at least in the foreseeable future. They know many children will start drinking as young as 4, 5, 6 - either with parents knowing, or not (by exploring cupboards when parents are out or asleep). Perhaps three words in this paragraph suggest a way forward - "foreseeable future" and "parents". As a more preventive-orientated policy towards Alcohol and Youth emerges which can be accepted and practised by youth, parents, teachers and maybe even drinks manufacturers (who have already found they can make enjoyable profit from alcohol-free drinks) society's attitude may change as it has with tobacco. Until then the most sensible policy would appear to be to discourage drinking by young people as far as possible, and supplement this with harm reduction information around:

- drinking and unsafe sex
- drinking and unsafe driving
- health consequences (physical, mental, emotional, spiritual, community)

Figure 8.1 indicates Harm Reduction being on tap, i.e. disseminated to known or suspected users only, from midway through primary school, principally but not exclusively with alcohol in mind. Tobacco will certainly come into significance with some children from age 8 or 9, and at the same age or little more, cannabis users are encountered now, and likely to be encountered in increasing numbers in future. Ironically, the Harm Reduction guidance for tobacco is Just Say No! For cannabis the information is the same, given that the most common method of ingestion is by smoking it with tobacco, and furthermore that cannabis is indicated to have even more carcinogens (cancer-causing agents) in it than tobacco, so much so that the onset of cancer can be faster in, say, a 5-a-day cannabis user than a 30-a-day tobacco user.

## Peer Education

Peer education is one of the coming things in Britain, and evaluators of peer prevention programmes in other countries show good results, often better than through any other prevention mode. We may be in danger of rushing fences here, though, and it is perhaps better to allow the technologies of Prevention (as distinct from Drug Education) and Peer Education to settle in somewhat, before trying to combine the two in Britain yet awhile.

Peer-based prevention programmes have a wonderful potential, on the evidence of (int. al.) arguably the most rigorous appraisal of US programmes. In 1986 Nancy Tobler published her "Meta-analysis of 143 Adolescent Drug Prevention Programmes". She found that for the average adolescent "peer programmes are dramatically more effective than all other programmes".

## Come Together, Right Now

Subsequent chapters show how teachers (9), peers (10), parents (11) and the community at large (12) can get involved in this process of prevention, and in doing so can get more involved with each other. Certainly, unless efforts are multi-disciplinal and unless old peer group or professional jealousies are laid aside the overall effect will at best be much reduced, at most be fatally injured.

Professional back-up should always be identified for rapid response when needed, as shown on the Contiguous Strategy illustrated in Figure 8.1. Your youth or adult prevention activities, especially confidential groupwork, may stir up issues or behaviours that need quick and practised support, if the person concerned is to be appropriately helped. Do not neglect this aspect - it is vitally important.

## How to Evaluate Materials

Rigorous evaluation of prevention or education materials is most probably a job for the specialist, but the lay reader or prevention practitioner can still make a workable judgement, based on more than subjectivity. One basis for evaluating programmes would be the listing in Chapter 6 - "Characteristics of Effective Prevention Programmes". Don't be too quick to jettison programmes which fail on some parameters; you may be able to supplement the programme without jeopardising it. Another basis, for the lay reader, would be to read the professional evaluations the specialist has produced; though the technology of evaluation may be beyond grasp, the evaluation report itself (usually) is not. There is no such thing as an unbiased evaluator, of course, but by careful study one can develop a working assessment method that will prevent your being diverted by evaluation bias.

One of the best collections of evaluations to come out in recent years is **OSAP Prevention Monograph 3**, published 1990. Sixteen papers cover a diverse range of evaluations. It may well be that the programme/process you are thinking of using is not explicitly covered in these papers, but you will gain many clues as to how to evaluate any product, wherever in the world it is produced.

Another American publication which could put you into excess baggage if you tried to carry it home is **Prevention Plus (PP) I and II**. Even the more recent volume Volume II weighs in at 541 quarto pages, and the final flyleaf threatens "In all likelihood there will be a Prevention Plus III". The PP books are a rich source of guidance in evaluating prevention materials.

Harking back to Chapter 1 of this book, the business of proving the effectiveness of programmes is technically difficult and can produce "Analysis-Paralysis". But take heart. The PP books, like OSAP Monograph 3, are not solely concerned with this high-powered end of evaluation; the lay prevention practitioner will find much to illuminate and guide.

There is, or certainly has been, a tendency in American social sciences to over-emphasise the "science" aspect and then be despondent when failing to clear an impossibly high hurdle. In her review, in PP II, of Peer Programmes, Bonnie Benard highlights this defeatist tendency. (Similar hari-kiri outlooks were observed by Professor Brian Sheldon, Social Studies Department, Royal Holloway & Bedford College, University of London, in his landmark paper "Social Work Effectiveness Experiments: Review and Implications" which covered American as well as British practice). The behavioural outcome was for researchers to "forcefully denounce entire programmes of professional practice". The baby repeatedly went out with the bathwater, and it is some measure of the validity of prevention that the baby kept coming back up the plughole for more. That resilience could not and cannot be explained by mere "religious faith in prevention", and indeed is now validated by technically more sensitive evaluations. But the validity was there all the time, perhaps best enunciated by Stanley Greenspan, an infant-development researcher. Stanley suggests we are getting the wrong answers because we have been asking the wrong questions; the decision to try prevention or not is one that "can be informed by, but will not be completely resolved by data". He illustrates this by a quote from an unnamed European researcher:

> "you Americans have a funny way of looking at evaluation. First you confuse research and politics. There are some things that are not research questions: that is, issues such as should there be equity in health care? These are basic questions of social philosophy that the country must answer - research can determine if this equity is taking place. But one does not research whether or not people should have a place to live or food to eat. In addition, in the United States you evaluate programs to decide whether or not to withdraw financial support. This differs from the attitude in much of Europe where the basic thrust of the program is assumed to be correct and the evaluation used to improve it, or to determine why it did not accomplish what it set out to do".

It is a fine irony that in 1985 Greenspan was exhorting US workers to follow the European line - to avoid neglecting good programmes through clumsy evaluation. Now here we Europeans are in 1992, using (or abusing) the American experience of evaluation to dismiss our indigenous approach to prevention!

It will be some time yet before this above described common-sense and intuition that powers the prevention practitioners are heavily supplemented by comprehensive evaluation research, but studies such as those by Schaps (1980) and Tobler (1986) light the way, and facilitate an impeccable defence of prevention as a practice, amply rebutting the criticism both by dedicated sceptics and by pro-drug crusaders.

## Evaluation Criteria for Programmes

Karol Kumpfer of the University of Utah suggests searching questions that could be asked in relation to a programme. These are shown in Figure 8.3. They make daunting reading. Nevertheless, having applied such criteria, Kumpfer expresses herself "optimistic that co-ordinated school-based programs can and do have a positive impact on youth and should be continued".

## PROGRAM EVALUATION QUESTIONS

1. What is the theoretical model underlying this program? Are intermediate, mediating variables measured to lend credence to the posited theoretical model? Could the ultimate outcomes of reduced drug use have been caused by external, uncontrolled factors?

2. What are the program objectives? Are they broken down into immediate program objectives (activities), intermediate client objectives, and ultimate client or community impact objectives? Are the objectives measurable, realistic, changeable within the program, and specific to the theoretical model for the targetted youth? A back-step analysis may help program planners determine where the most cost-effective point would be to interrupt a causal chain of hypothesised factors that lead to use or abuse.

3. Were process data collected to tell whether the program was implemented as planned? Program evaluations of good model programs may show poor results, not because the model programme is worthless, but because it was not implemented as designed.

4. Is the sample of sufficient size to permit reasonable confidence in the research results? Knowledge of confidence intervals helps here.

5. Is the sample representative of the student body with all groups included? Generally this means a random sample of all students in the school with a high participation rate of 80 per cent or more of those randomly selected. If high- risk students are omitted, then the sample is biased.

6. Is there differential attrition at the post-test with more of the high risk students dropping out of the sample because of moving away or dropping out of school? If so the improvements may be due simply to fewer using students in the post-test sample.

7. Are the test instruments reliable and valid? Are there repeated questions to check for consistency in answers? Are standardised and normed scales or tests included in the test battery? Are demographic data included to determine the effect of the program for different types of students?

**Figure 8.3 (Part 1) Programme Evaluation Criteria**

## PROGRAM EVALUATION QUESTIONS

8. Are the data collection techniques standardised and protected from potential bias? What percentage of missing data occured? How many completed tests had to be omitted because students could not read, could not understand the questions, or chose not to answer many of the questions accurately?

9. Is there triangulation of data sources? In other words have several different people (i.e. students, teachers, administrators, parents, independent observers and so forth) been asked for information on the same variables?

10. How cost-effective is this program? How many students (numbers, not percentages) were stopped from becoming users and/or abusers and for how long? A program touting a 50 per cent reduction in initiation may be talking about keeping small numbers (say 2 from 20) from initiating use for 1 year. Is this worth the cost to the taxpayer?

11. Are there control groups to check for baseline changes in matched students? Some programs show very few positive changes when compared to natural improvements due to other community changes. Other programs may look like failures because more youth were using drugs at the post-test. However, when compared to control schools, the experimental programs actually may have prevented more students from using.

12. What is the effect size and significance of the results? Does a statistically significant difference translate into the changes in measured variables of sufficient size to warrant replication of the program?

13. What happens to the high-risk students and the current users after this program is implemented? Hence, what are the real cost savings to society if this program is implemented?

**Figure 8.3 (Part 2) Programme Evaluation Criteria**

The National Federation of Parents puts its criteria in more digestible language. To the NFP, effective curricula include:

- up to date and accurate drug intelligence
- rejection of "responsible use" messages
- abstinence below 21 for drugs and alcohol
- comprehensiveness, and continuity from nursery to end of school years (and beyond)
- readability at each age
- completeness at each year level, leading naturally to the next year
- upbeat, appealing presentation
- skills in gathering/evaluating information
- decision making, coping, self concept, peer pressure reversal
- discussion of school policies on drugs
- ease of updating. Publisher to commit to updates
- flexibility, for varying educational settings
- teacher training and updates
- evaluation
- student/parent/teacher input to design
- parent education
- promotion of parent/community action
- use of community resources
- encouragement of peer-teaching, drug-free youth groups, etc.
- alcohol as well as other drugs
- all stages of drug use, not just "addiction"
- ease of integration into school curriculum and other subjects such as English, Science, Maths, etc. - compatibility with health education, personal and social education, etc.
- no shortage of materials for teacher
- adequate reference back-up for teacher
- avoidance of "curiosity-builders" such as drug-taking technique illustrations
- cultural sensitivity. Flexibility to meet individual needs
- exploitation of hot news issues
- addressing media issues, overt/covert/implied/subliminal approval of drug use ( - songs. movies, commercials, teeshirts, cartoons, etc.)
- use of visual, auditory and kinesthetic learning
- use of interactive, experiential learning
- knowledge, attitudes and behaviour

The Utah and NFP lists should give any parent or educator or governor ample facility to assess and select the best programme or programmes for the school. Some American schools include pupils on the selection committee for drug education/prevention materials. Selection of programmes is a major exercise but there are many other items to consider.

## Evaluation Criteria for Materials

The following is based on research by the Committees of Correspondence, a Massachusetts-based watchdog (of the Rottweiler variety) dedicated to identifying and blocking pro-drug jargon in the literature and also the media. C of C organiser Otto Moulton is a wonderful character, a no-nonsense, blunt but humorous speaker who handed his million dollar business over to his children so he and his wife Connie could concentrate full time on drug prevention. Otto's recommendations for youth drug prevention material are:

### Check date of publication

If from late 70s/early 80s it is probably out of date unless revised. (There will be exceptions.) Don't be fooled by recent publication/copyright dates.

### Research the authors' affiliations

Membership of NORML, Drug Policy Foundation (or in Britain, being on the editorial board of the International Journal of Drug Policy) indicates that a jaundiced view of prevention is likely.

### Ensure current, accurate drug facts

Latest information on harmfulness of cannabis is important; the standard ISDD output ("There is no conclusive evidence that long term cannabis use causes physical dependence, or lasting physical or mental damage") is now several years out of date. Note the avoidance of reference to psychological dependence, often a lot tougher to break. The bibliography of the University of Mississippi lists more than 9,000 papers testifying to the harmfulness of cannabis, all published since 1965. Cocaine is addictive. Alcohol is a drug.

### Be alert for contradictory messages

Some publications purport to give a scientific appraisal of drug use, but in fact are either voyeuristic indulgent journalism, or, as with Arnold Trebach and company, are pro-drug argument dressed up as "the Search for Truth".

**Clear and unequivocal message**
No unlawful use of alcohol or other drugs.

**Promote positive standards of behaviour**
Provide information to reinforce a young person's courage to stay drug-free. Teach people of all ages, especially youths, to make decisions for which they are responsible and accountable.

**Focus on reasons not to use drugs**
Or, to put it better, focus on benefits of a drug-free lifestyle.

**Video/film material**
Video is the medium of choice for youth. The message must be clearly drug- free and promote this lifestyle. Realistic settings are more effective; young people respond best when real people, places, events are on the screen. They understand that actors deal in fantasy, therefore they may not react to a message that involves actors, fictional script, cartoons, or other "showbiz" trappings.

Credible communicators are very important to acceptance of the message. Youth like hearing from drug-free youth role models. Health issues come across best from doctors or health professionals. Legal consequences of drug use come best from a uniformed police officer (in the US setting). The usual reservations as to using recovering drug users apply, i.e. it is fatally easy to convey the suggestion that everyone can come through an episode of drug abuse and look as hale and hearty as this person. This may be true for some people, but it can prompt the thought, especially in younger viewers, that they could get away with it too (which may be proved sadly wrong). Avoid films that dwell on or glamourise former users.

Films produced by qualified drug prevention writers are worth short-listing. Films that demonstrate the consequences of use are vital to the psychology of prevention, but this should be kept in perspective. "Shock-horror" such as the old British Police movie "Better Dead" has now been widely panned as counter-productive. Having said this, incontestible facts about damage (physical/mental/emotional/spiritual/social) resulting from drugs are a valid element, provided always that the presenter does not soporifically drone on about it. Keep it in proportion.

Films giving explicit scenes of drug use are a no-no. They can "open a Pandora's box of mixed messages - on one hand, DON'T and on the other HERE'S HOW". Some films of this nature are intended as training films for drug professionals or for teachers, parents, etc. In that setting, such scenes may be fair enough, but if you purchase them, mark them clearly as "Not for screening to youth".

Be cautious about films that lack depth. Films should do more than superficially urge youth to "say no" to drugs; they must give the student sufficient motivation to opt to be drug-free, show how to tactfully avoid drugs, and suggest practical and attractive alternatives. There should be no accusation or confrontation of attitudes, i.e. no using the video/film as a soapbox from which to deliver propaganda. This tends to be an automatic turn-off. The presentation should confine itself to objective facts and consequences of drug use, in comparison with drug-free life.

**Weasel Words**

Identifying "strategic semantics" is one of the Committees of Correspondence specialisations, and Otto has traced several of the nuggets of jargon given below back to the pro-drug lobbies. Although this listing is derived from American experience, it is illuminating to see how many of the phrases are today firmly rooted in British culture... perhaps your first task should be to weed your patch!

Watch out for "warning flag" PHRASES:

EXPERIMENTAL USE Drug users do not experiment with drugs as a scientist experiments with substances in the laboratory.

RECREATIONAL USE The word "recreation" means doing something healthy. Using drugs is NOT an acceptable form of recreation.

SOCIAL USE Drugs are anti-social and destroy families, friendships and social interaction.

"SOFT" DRUGS No illegal drug is "soft" on the body. This adjective implies harmlessness.

MOOD-ALTERING The implication is that only temporary feelings are involved when, in fact, what causes these moods are biological changes in the brain. The term used should be "mind-altering".

USE/ABUSE/MISUSE This implies that USE is okay but ABUSE should be avoided. Any use of illegal drugs IS abuse.

CONTROLLED USE There is no quality control in the contents of illegal drugs. Their addictive qualities lead to uncontrolled use.

RESPONSIBLE USE The use of illegal drugs is irresponsible, harmful to health and NEVER responsible. Judgements and perceptions are impaired when using any psychoactive drug. After using a psychoactive substance, one cannot make a "responsible" decision.

LUMPING TOGETHER UNLIKE SUBSTANCES A common ploy of the drug culture is comparing medications, aspirin, caffeine, or chocolate with illegal mind-altering drugs. There is a vast difference, and this approach minimizes the difference between legal and illegal substances and gives a message that dangerous drugs have a benign quality.

"THERE ARE NO GOOD OR BAD DRUGS, JUST IMPROPER USE" This expression is found in pro-drug literature which confuses the reader and minimizes the distinct chemical differences among substances. Clarification is needed to differentiate between prescription medicines and illicit drugs.

"IT'S YOUR DECISION" "Now that you know the facts, it's your choice whether or not to use illegal drugs". In what other area do we teach our children, "It's your choice to break the law?". Decisions that break the law are unacceptable. Everyone should make decisions for which they are responsible and accountable.

SCARE TACTICS Scientific research results are NOT scare tactics. Facts are facts. Carefully interpret statistics. Commonly-used percentages can be misleading, i.e.: 50% of 2 is vastly different than 50% of 1000. Check author, date and number of people tested.

INDIVIDUAL RIGHTS Legal rights do NOT pertain to ILLEGAL activity.

"WHAT LITTLE WE KNOW" or "LITTLE IS KNOWN" Since 1965, over 9,399 scientific research papers on marijuana have been published and are listed in **An Annotated Bibliography of Marijuana Volumes I & II and Supplements**, available from the University of Mississippi Research Institute of Pharmaceutical Sciences. All reports state that marijuana is harmful to health.

# CHAPTER 9

# TEACHER POWER

Teachers in Britain have "had it up to here". Fruitless industrial action in the 80s left them feeling impotent, a feeling reinforced by changes to their negotiating structure which transferred more power to central Government. Similar transfer of power was a consequence of the introduction of the National Curriculum, and teachers struggling to come to terms with this fundamental restructuring - having not long since wrestled with the remodelling of GCE examination systems into GCSE - were now additionally burdened with Attainment Target measuring.

For Health (Drug) Education Coordinators this produced stony ground in which to sow any drug prevention seeds. Not only were the teachers demoralised and over-stretched, the constraints of the National Curriculum tended to marginalise this vital subject.

The only place in which drugs were specifically listed was in the Science curriculum. Not the best environment for exploring feelings, emotions, and the like. Curriculum Guidance 5 (Health Education) related to drugs inter alia, but this is an advisory, i.e. not a mandatory document. The good news is that Government did in due course confirm the vital importance of Health Education, and proposed that it would best be dealt with in a "cross- curricular" manner. Thus, mathematics lessons would work out the profit on a kilo of heroin cut with 90% brick dust and sold in gram wraps with a 400% mark-up. Language lessons would teach one to say "Help. My wallet has been appropriated by a woman bearing the hallmarks of amphetamine psychosis". And this is supposed to prevent drug use... Another concern is that cross-curricular dissemination of prevention is analogous to taking a small knob of butter and spreading it across many pieces of toast; everyone agrees it's on there, but no one can taste it. Cynicism aside, there are potentially solid benefits in cross-curricular work, and as this book has demonstrated the whole subject of prevention is much more diverse than the kind of substance-specific examples used above. Witness the following extract from National Curriculum Council Guidance (CG3):

> "...the Education Reform Act (1988) places a statutory responsibilty on schools to provide a broad and balanced curriculum which promotes the spirtual, moral, cultural, mental and physical development of pupils at the school and of society; and also prepares pupils for the opportunities, responsibilities and experiences of adult life."

But the main concern has to be that whilst it is relatively simple to transmit "Knowledge" in a cross-curricular format, how one deals with affective education, with influencing "Attitudes" and "Behaviour", whilst utilising largely didactic academic subject teaching methods must be difficult in the extreme. Benjamin Bloom in his classic text on the "taxonomy" of learning assessed that only 4% of school time can be said to comprise affective education. The solution that comes readily to mind is to use the "Tribes" Co-operative Learning model (see Chapter 4) as a basis. But this is only a basis; time is still needed, time dedicated specifically for this vital subject.

What prevention really needs in addition to cross-curricular work and the Tribes model, is a slot of its own within the health education programme, which in turn needs its own defined, protected and less abused place in the timetable; not used as a repository for low-rated teachings by low-rated teachers. If we can get prevention (and health education generally) right, so much else will follow. It therefore demands the best of teaching by the best of teachers.

## Attainment Targets

Speaking of the best of teaching, and as we are now in the age of Attainment Targets, perhaps it would be useful to attempt some schedules of year-by-year attainments for drug education/prevention. These are modified by the author to suit British culture, being drawn from two sources; the National Federation of Parents, and the Department of Education in conjunction with the Office of Substance Abuse Prevention.

Figures 9.1 to 9.4 offer attainment targets for the British culture. These are not pious or "pie in the sky" artificialities. These are real targets used by real schools. If you are serious about prevention (and to have read this far you must be), then you should take these targets seriously.

These attainment target schedules are of course only a skeletal framework for developing a curriculum in your school or unit. A considerable amount of amplification is needed to produce the finished article, and whilst much of what is either stated herein or listed in the references will be of help, there is a need to rationalise this material and make it applicable to the British educational culture. A further publication meeting this need is under production now. See reference list for details.

**Salespersonship**

Figure 9.5 is to help you convince seniors that Prevention has multiple benefits. Academic improvement and teacher de-stressing are just two of the many spin-offs; all of the negative aspects on the outer 'gearwheel' will be beneficially affected by a comprehensive prevention programme.

**ATTAINMENT SPECIFICS 5 - 8 Years of Age**

By 8 years of age or sooner they should be able to:

* Recognise that they are unique and special.
* Understand the need for and effects of rest, exercise and food on the way we feel.
* Identify harmful substances in the environment.
* Distinguish betwen medicines and harmful substances.
* Understand from whom it is safe to take medicines.
* Identify different feelings and realise they can make people behave differently.
* Accept that when people have problems it is alright to ask for help.
* Know that they can influence the feelings of others.
* Realise the need for rules and sharing and understand consequences of ignoring rules.
* Work on developing friendships and understand validation.

Sources: OSAP/Dept. of Education
NFP Curriculum & Resource Review
Author research

**Figure 9.1 Attainment targets**

**ATTAINMENT SPECIFICS 9 - 11 Years of Age**

By 11 years of age or sooner they should be able to:

* Understand the individual's responsibility for caring for themselves and their own health.

* Summarise how drugs can affect the body and how some drugs are mind-altering.

* Classify commonly found substances which could be harmful if used inappropriately.

* Recognise peer group pressure in a variety of situations.

* Be able to identify and practise peer pressure reversal skills.

* Understand how to retain individuality in a group setting.

* List negative effects of tobacco, solvents, alcohol and cannabis.

* Understand simple decision-making processes and the short- and long-term effects of decisions.

* List healthy ways of dealing with stressful feelings.

* Understand the importance of helping others.

* Understand the importance of self-esteem.

* Have a clear understanding of the facts of life and be aware of the various sexually transmitted diseases.

Sources: OSAP/Dept. of Education
NFP Curriculum & Resource Review
Author research

**Figure 9.2 Attainment targets**

**ATTAINMENT SPECIFICS 12 - 14 Years of Age**

By 14 years of age or sooner they should be able to:

* Acknowledge and measure the importance of family ties.

* Understand the effect of group influences on personal values, beliefs and behaviour.

* List consequences of risk-taking behaviour.

* State the effects of drugs on the human body.

* Recognise and understand the terms drug dependence, legal and illegal drugs drug tolerance, prescription drugs, psychoactive drugs, street drugs.

* Understand the laws regarding drug use.

* Assess media messages on TV, film, music, cinema, adverts.

* Be able to discuss and acknowledge sexuality and to recognise the connection between sexual behaviour and HIV, and other sexually-transmitted diseases.

Sources: OSAP/Dept. of Education
NFP Curriculum & Resource Review
Author research

**Figure 9.3 Attainment targets**

**ATTAINMENT SPECIFICS 15 - 18 Years of Age**

By 18 years of age or sooner they should be able to:

* Understand harmful effects of drugs, including alcohol, on unborn children.

* State potential positive and negative social, economic, physical, psychological, legal and effects of drugs on individuals and society.

* Identify proper names and street names for commonly abused drugs, list the long- and short-term effects of each.

* Understand the various routes to HIV infection, and understand more fully sexuality and sexual behaviour, including sexual orienta tion.

* Understand the myths and stereotypes which surround drug use.

* State the reasons why some people choose to use or not use drugs.

* Understand the dangers of passive smoking and the hazards of smoking to health.

* Understand the blood/alcohol limits for safe driving, the reasons for abstinence when driving, and also the effects of other drugs on driving.

* Suggest how drug use can affect financial affairs.

* Recognise the importance of healthy coping mechanisms in times of crisis.

* List healthy alternatives to getting high on drugs or alcohol.

Sources: OSAP/Dept. of Education
NFP Curriculum & Resource Review
Author research

**Figure 9.4 Attainment Targets**

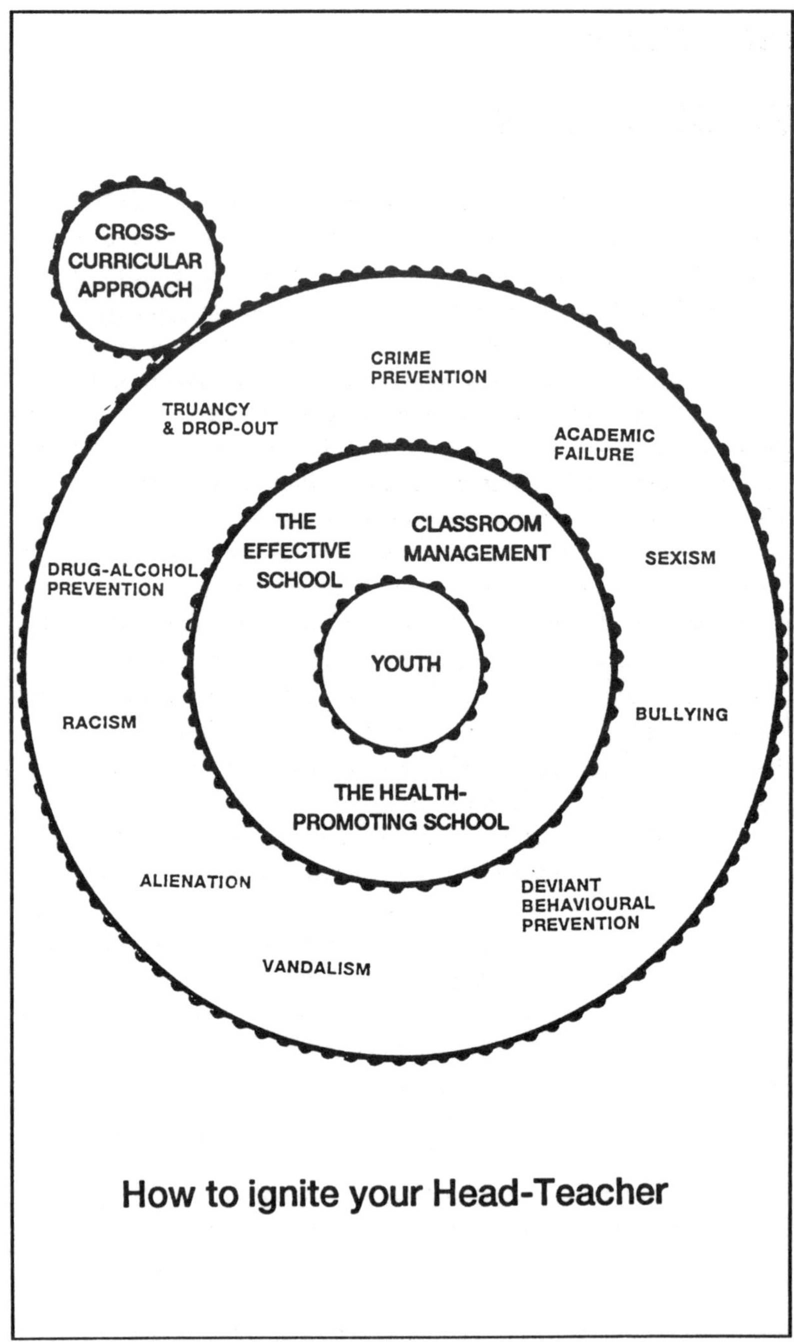


**Figure 9.5 Gearing Up for Prevention (& PSE)**

# CHAPTER 10

# PEER POWER

Peer education is the coming thing in Britain. Conferences are being held; articles published; policies formulated; directives drafted... meanwhile off to one side the youths themselves enquire as to when they get to join in, and are told to "Shut up and wait over there. You'll hear when it's time!".

In actuality sincere efforts are being put into youth involvement as a precursor to peer education per se, but such a radical departure deserves to be taken steadily, and with a substantial adult contingent in the steering group. The incentive to pressing ahead with peer education is, of course, the inspirational results observed in other countries; process and outcome achievements have been most encouraging.

Nancy Tobler's classic meta analysis in 1986 was a great spur to the movement, but not the first. Nilsen - Geibel's observations of the prevention benefits of peer groups in West Germany dates back to 1980. Here in Britain Dr. Harith Swadi, adolescent and child psychiatrist has conducted several researches into drug abuse; of these, two are particularly germane. In 1988 he co-authored "Peer influence and adolescent substance abuse: a promising side", then in the same year he produced "Adolescent drug-taking: role of family and peers".

Whilst these and other academics were slaving over hot theories, the field workers were pressing ahead with the practice. The Teenex programme was in some ways designed to mate with the Tribes programme; one is extramural (Teenex) and the other school-based. Both encourage peer empowerment, and both use interactive/experiential learning methods including group work using very similar norms. Because Tribes in its early phases in Britain is more readily taken on by lower school (or even primary), whilst Teenex is for upper-school age, the combined approach fits together well to provide an exemplary peer education package. Graduates from the Teenex programme (typically years 11 - 13) have been working with year 7 pupils in two schools in West London. The younger pupils seem to welcome the classes, and teachers who have observed the process are very enthusiastic. This process is now being fostered in another school in Berkshire.

A future objective, when Teenex programme throughput increases the number of graduates to more sustainable levels, is to develop presentation teams on the PRIDE model. These teams go into schools by arrangement with teaching staff and work all day on various aspects of drugs with "a sizeable number" of pupils. At day's end the pupils have learned a lot and also devised a show which is presented that evening to parents and staff demonstrating their learning. The cultural transferability of this programme has been demonstrated in Britain for four years now by the Teenex end-of-training shows.

The above is in addition to other in-school "peer education" in the widest sense by Teenex graduates. They are also expected to be informed ambassadors and role leaders for a drug-free lifestyle (but not preachers). Other expectations include presentations to classmates or, as a group of Teenexers, to year groups or even whole school. Other presentations which have happened in addition to all of the above are to parents and governors, or to Local Authority appointed or elected members. One such notable event was ignited when a worried parent asked the thirteen fresh-faced and healthy-looking youth on the stage "How many of you have ever been offered drugs?" On a count of three (to avoid peer pressure) those experiencing offers took a pace forward. Only two were left at the rear. The powerful impact of this simple communication led to the creation of an active parents group in that school and parental involvement in Teenex.

Another key development from the Teenex programme has been the emergence of peer counsellors. This was a formalisation of something that was happening anyway, after Teenex camps; the graduates were finding that their improved self-assurance coupled with warmth, led several pupils to gravitate towards them, to find a listening ear. The school grapevine, letting people know exactly who had been on a drug training camp, also prompted people with concerns to look out for the peer counsellor. Those considered adequately qualified through Teenex and supplementary training were given a badge to signify their status. The practice throughout was to use the peer counsellors as a first point of contact only; no one was suggesting that peer counsellors could match the skills of a trained and qualified adult counsellor; the peer counsellors are more akin to Befrienders (see British Association of Counselling definition) and are always backed up by qualified adult counsellors.

A programme which has been running in or around British schools for years is Young Enterprise; in this scheme young people assisted by adult advisers run a small company, including product design/manufacture/sales. The youths occupy all the senior officer parts. This concept has been extended to Crime Concern, except this time the product is crime prevention. Prosaic activities like identity marking and bicycle theft give way to more ambitious projects like bullying and drug/alcohol abuse. The accent is on prevention rather than detection. Crime Concern is based in Swindon, and help from them is readily forthcoming.

A brief mention is justified, in the context of peer support, of two existing programmes in Britain that have used peer groups to help with the stresses caused by alcohol or other drug abuse; they are Alateen and Families Anonymous respectively. Part of the AA family, they apply the "12-step" process to caring for the young relatives of abusers.

# CHAPTER 11

# PARENT POWER

> "The nice thing about America is the way the parents obey their children."
>
> (Anon)

Whilst there has been an upsurge in the importance attached to peer education in Britain there is no corresponding advance in recognition of the value of parent initiatives, either singly or in groups. Perhaps this is because the peer education work is largely (though not exclusively) rooted inside the school gates, whereas the parents are on the outside looking in. Another, more regrettable reason is that, in the main, British parents have yet to wake up. Even when the message is loud and clear enough to break the slumber, the next affliction is deafness, followed by denial. Moreover, those few in the audience who are by nature activists are likely already overburdened with worthy causes. But parents are vital to this defence of their most precious asset, their children.

The parent movement in America can take a sizeable slice of the credit for the improvements in drug prevention over the last 10-12 years. It is no injustice that the biggest prevention organisation in the US is named the **Parents** Resource Institute (PRIDE). Cultural differences between here and there have some bearing; Americans do seem to be "joiners" by nature, much more so than Britons. But countless campaigns in the past and even now (such as the opposition to the Channel Tunnel High Speed Link) show that British communities are capable of mobilising and showing stamina.

It is the task of the prevention worker to deliver that spark which ignites significant parent action. Liverpool showed how it could be done, although this was for a more clearly defined target, in that the campaign was to help already involved users; Joan Keogh's Parents Against Drug Abuse (PADA) is a model of its kind and did great things to improve Liverpool's resources for users. But Joan's community was painfully racked with a substantial degree of heavy-end drug use, with a high prevalence of injecting heroin users. Joan's own family was affected, spurring her on to greater efforts. Is this really the situation we want to reach in Britain at large before parent power comes alive?

Turning to the positive aspects of parent power, feeling disabled by ignorance is an illusion. You do not need to be an expert to begin (or continue) your constructive contribution to prevention. For a start there are simple measures that any family can take to reduce the possibility of drug involvement. Take the parameters humourously outlined in Figure 11.1 and turn them on their head. This won't guarantee you a drug-free household but it will certainly help. Some of the improvements you may experience are what are called "process goals" rather than "outcome". For example, if in future you were to eat together as a family this might, hopefully be a prop to the structure of a drug-free existence, but at the very least would be an enrichment of your family life.

No one should imagine that studying the subject produces a force-field that blocks out all chance of drug abuse. Bill and Nancy Perkins found this out to their cost when they failed to spot that one of their five children was involved. This in spite of their being certified drug and alcohol counsellors who had learnt "the hard way", as recovering alcoholics. Their reactions of anger, confusion, fear, instability were just like any other family. How they won through is absorbingly told in their book "Raising Drug Free Kids in a Drug Filled World". Many valuable prevention lessons here.

Two other mothers, with three children each, are Adele Faber and Elaine Mazlish. They have produced a little gem of a book around one of the key correlates with drug abuse: communications. It has a superb title: "How to Talk so Kids will Listen & Listen so Kids will Talk" and an even more superb opening line ... "I was a wonderful parent before I had children". (A salutory remark for many a Health Educator!) This book has already helped over 15,000 parents groups improve their family communications skills, and should help you too.

While we seem to be in a bookish mode there is another which is a little specialised but persevere with it, for it will be a great experience. No, it isn't "Fly Fishing" by J. R. Hartley, it is "Games People Play" by Eric Berne, and it illuminates something called Transactional Analysis. In brief, this describes how in each of us there is a Parent, an Adult, and a Child. The parent is authoritarian, patriarchal; the adult rational and flexible; the child potentially good or naughty, wilful, joyful, demanding and manipulative. Whichever mode we are in when we start a communication may well affect the mode the other person assumes. Age is irrelevant. If you go into Child the other person is likely to go Parent, and vice versa. Child-Child is for fun. Adult-Adult is for rational discourse. There's much more to it than this, of course, and for a "sequel" relevant to drug prevention read Claude Steiner's "Games Alcoholics Play", also "I'm OK, You're OK" by Thomas A. Harris, which is in the same genre.

**SIXTEEN TESTED WAYS TO ENCOURAGE YOUR CHILD TO USE DRUGS**

1. Never eat together as a family.
2. Never have family traditions which occur weekly, monthly, or annually that children can look forward to.
3. Never listen to your children - talk at them but not with them.
4. Never let your children experience cold, fatigue, adventure, injury, risk, challenge, experimentation, failure, frustration, discouragement, etc.,
5. Teach them to "do as I say - not as I do".
6. Leave the responsibility of spiritual training and development to the schools and church, but don't teach them at home.
7. When confronted with the choice of whether spending your time or money on a material pursuit or on a family activity, always choose the material.
8. Expect your child to achieve, to win, but don't teach him the principles of life, of living. Let him learn them on his own.
9. Take a "pick up pill" in the morning followed by a "relaxant" at night.
10. Never correct your children appropriately, but uphold them before the law, school, church and friends as "not my **little** boy."
11. Undermine the role of the father in the home - never have the father's influence in the home - stay together for the sake of the children - or better yet get a divorce.
12. Always pick up after him, never let him take responsibility.
13. Keep your home atmosphere in a state of chaos.
14. Always solve his problems - make his decisions.
15. Be too busy with business, civic or social life to spend time with your children. Or, if you do happen to have time, spend it together ... watching television.
16. Don't teach them while they are young. Wait until they are old enough to learn and decide right or wrong for themselves.

Source: PRIDE Conference 87

**Figure 11.1 Drug Promotion for Parents**

Parent power, as the above publications show, does not mean all-powerful patriachs any more than peer power means the corollorary. The optimum situation means the Empowered Family, each member empowered by their personal lifeskills and enlightenment to act in a way which promotes their own well being whilst respecting the rights of others and recognising the consequences of actions... the downstream benefit in drug prevention terms is well worth it, and for the process goals alone the exercise is highly justified.

Start, then, with your own family and, if it needs it, strengthen it with these and other techniques. The time to look beyond your home to parent groups and community groups is when you are confident in your family's stability. If you are heading out to help others rather than face your own family situation, you may need to think this one through again. Training for parent groups can be part D-I-Y, part by inviting various specialists. Chapters 4 and 5 give relevant information - or write to this author for more information.

There is no need to take space in this book with advice on how to run a pressure group. Go and talk to someone who is running one locally; the topic they will be pursuing is relatively unimportant since most roles, strategies and tactics translate from one topic to another. (One of the best texts on the subject "How to Run a Pressure Group" by former CPRE Director Christopher Hall is unfortunately now out of print.) Why a pressure group? Because you will inevitably be involved in campaigning, for wider acceptance and support, for resources and funds, and in converting people to your point of view. These people will include school staff, parent-governors associations (which you should try to join), police, councillors, youth workers and of course parents thus far more apathetic than you.

You may even have to enter into dialogue with your local drug educationalist or health education professionals, if you find that the message they are promoting is at odds with yours. (See Chapter 3 for some thoughts on this.) Do not assume they have got it right or that they are unbiased, because of the role they occupy. Respect for professional experience and expertise takes a person so far in dialogues, but the subject under consideration here is risky behaviour by the charges of parents, i.e. your children. It is not pure mathematics, it is not an exact science, and it impacts your life directly. It is, therefore, in order for you to study the matter rationally, from your standpoint out there in the grass roots, then respectfully and responsibly but firmly demonstrate to anyone who has an influence on your child exactly what is meant by parent power.

Good luck!

# CHAPTER 12

# COMMUNITY POWER

With the arguable exception of Chapters 8 and 9 (arguable because reading them will give any "community " i.e "out of school" person a better idea of how to integrate with school-based prevention) the whole of this second section is relevant to developing community power. Without whole- community involvement the impact of your programme will be seriously undermined.

## Exactly Who has a Role, and What?

One of the best graphic models answering this question was developed by Texans' War on Drugs and is shown as Figure 12.1. Whilst for any given community one might want to modify the organisations listed, the basic model holds good anywhere. The position of organisations on the target can also be changed to suit your community, since the principle is that the closer to the bullseye, i.e. youth, the greater the potential influence. Once again, there are basic truths, such as the proximity to the bullseye of family and school, which are likely to be valid anywhere.

A further useful feature of the Texan target model is that it can be used as a progress measurement tool. If a transparent overlay is marked up, one can see how the work of community mobilisation is progressing. If there are irregularities on the shape of the overlay this indicates a shortcoming that needs rectification. And by the way, in the excitement of making contact with groups all over town, don't forget to make contact with the group **in** the bullseye!

The Texan bullseye target gives a starting plan for your campaign. In looking at this plan it is important to recognise that the community as a whole is made up of several distinct sub-groups, usually also called "communities". Thus, there is the Business Community, the School/s Community, the Sports Community, the Legal Community, the Media Community, and the Community at Large. (Alright so far?)

The concept of treating a whole school as a community has already been addressed in Chapter 8. Consistency of approach in every department is the key as indeed it is for all communities.

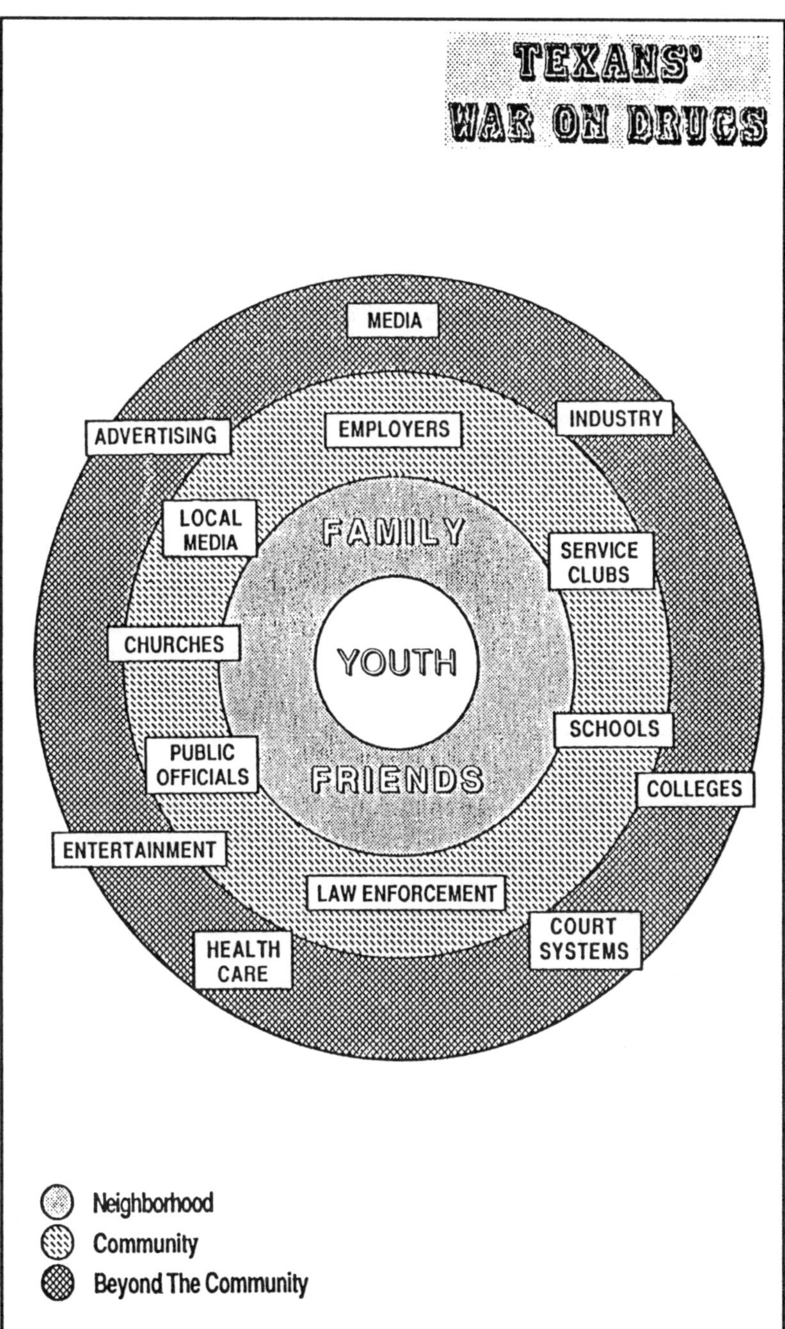


**Figure 12.1 Lone Star Community Development**

**Business: Issues and Rights**

The Business Community matters in many respects. We all suffer by paying too much for our everyday commodities, because British business is estimated to lose £4,000,000,000 per year as a result of drug and alcohol abuse. Some losses are spectacular - wrecked machinery or (perhaps) lost ships or planes. And sometimes dead or maimed people. But much of the loss is subtle; the half days at low production after liquid lunches, the few days off sick after a binge on sulphates or E at raves.

In struggling to come to terms with the fact that "if you have drugs in your country you have drugs in your company" British companies are, in the main, some years behind their USA (and Australian int. al.) counterparts. Some have had workplace alcohol policies for some time - the breweries and distilleries, for example, but this falls far short of a comprehensive EAP (Employee Assistance Programme) as described in Chapter 4 and even then most EAP's are a response strategy, not a prevention strategy. Denial is as inherent in the business world as it is in education, and both sectors need to learn the positive social and Cost-Benefit returns which stem from effective prevention. Employees, it has been found, usually wish to remain employees, and this is a powerful lever easing them into EAP commitment. Employers naturally comprehend this nexus, but are slow as anyone to grasp the benefits of prevention.

An effective company approach to drug and alcohol use would be to have an EAP including a prevention ("health promotion") programme in place, all of this being either individual for larger companies or shared for smaller companies. The indications from America are that a CBA ratio of anything from 4:1 to 18:1 applies, i.e.: for every pound you spend you get four pounds back and maybe much more. As a stepping stone to EAP there are ECS - Employee Counselling Services. These are narrower in scope, more focused to 'problems' than to advising or helping to improve the quality of the employee's life in general. Cheaper to run, but you get what you pay for!

There is a shift in attitude that comes from a company's involvement in EAP and health promotion, and in part this may be described as a greater "sense of community" which at its best affects everyone, from top to bottom. This sense of community is what any prevention group should strive to instil in every sector. Part of that sense should concern how, for example, your business community relates to the community at large. Everyday, but fun instances might be to ensure your company has a float in the local carnival, or to enter teams in sports leagues. Even in recession these activities can be a good return on investment. More formal instances could include involvement in education schemes like TVEI - Technical & Vocational Education Initiative, which give school pupils real insight into business (and vice versa), or Crime Concern; the youth crime prevention panels which need business advisers and may tackle drug/alcohol abuse or prevention, or both. Of course if there is a community drug prevention body your company's representation on this would be very welcome.

The essence then, for businesses, is that handing out funds for other bodies to tackle the problems is one part - and a gratefully received part of the whole solution. But much greater promise lies in real **involvement** by a business, involvement in prevention within its own "community", within the local business community, and within the community at large.

## Good Sports

The automatic concept when sports is mentioned in relation to drug prevention is to think of sports heroes as role models. This has however, proved a rocky road. The megastar you pick today, tomorrow may have feet of clay. A safer bet might be to promote sports as part of a healthy lifestyle in which drugs are unnecessary and harmful. Moreover sports can be a source of risk-taking, achievement, pleasure and self-esteem; in other words a good alternative to drugs.

Sports do have one disadvantage that business in the main does not, i.e. media scrutiny. Could business survive under the sort of observation implicit in a current advert for the 1992 Barcelona Olympics ... "the colours worn by the **10,000** sportsmen and women ... the colours that will be captured by the **11,000** journalists ...".(!) Imagine the news pages if the "winners" in an office promotion review had to be urine-tested under the eyes of a newspaper hack.

The result of this scrutiny has been the exposure of drug abuse in wide areas of sport; steroids, beta-blockers, amphetamines, cocaine; all these and more have been in use to go faster, be more accurate or, in both senses of the word, get higher. On top of this, sportsmen and women are members of everyday life and thus just as prone to abusing legal or illegal substances as any other mortal. In the experience of this author (who has played sport at representative level) there are three distinct blocks to progress within and around the Sports Community:

(1) The elitist nature of the activity militates against doing anything that interfaces with the common herd.

(2) The patriarchal style of too many sports administrators tends towards instructing sports players what/what not to do, and testing to ensure they comply. This is not a good atmosphere for developing prevention dialogue between sports players, nor does it facilitate a sense of internal or wider community.

(3) Denial and cynicism around drug use exists in sport as much as anywhere, perhaps the more so in the light of its tarnished image. Because of this even ostensibly 'clean' sports are reluctant to be involved in prevention, in case it should be thought that this means their sport has a drug problem.

None of these three blocks is immoveable. They all have to do with attitude, and with even the slightest lubricant of enlightenment they can be slid to one side.

Sport has a great deal to offer in the context of health promotion, and a great deal to gain from the community around it in terms of prevention, support and life enrichment. There is nothing wrong with an elitism based on sound parameters; this gives us all something to strive for. But that elitism needs to be tempered with humanity, to the benefit of all the sportspeople and the wider community they inhabit.

## The Case for the Law

Much of the legal side of the drugs subject has to do with response rather than prevention. Apprehending offenders, finding/imprisoning/probation-ordering/community-service-ordering of them. This typically involves magistrates, judges, court officials, probation officers, social workers, drug agencies and - of course - the police. There is a deterrent component to this activity, a demand reduction effect, in that some people refrain from drug/alcohol abuse rather than risk the legal consequences.

Not everything is deterrent-based, though. The police have a good record of crime prevention, some of it being under the "obstruct, hinder" meaning of the word, some of it definitely in the sense of "to come before" (praevenire). In this country, initiatives like Crime Concern have a sizeable primary prevention component.

Whilst Crime Concern is for secondary school, perhaps the greatest potential for police involvement is at primary level - and similarly in junior youth clubs. A uniformed officer is generally well - received in most British primary classrooms, (the same sadly cannot be said at the secondary level). In America several schemes involve police officers; the best known is DARE (Drug Abuse Prevention Education), born in Los Angeles in 1983 but now in 49 states, Canada, Australia, New Zealand, Samoa and Forces Schools worldwide. In 1990 alone the programmed audience was 4.5 million pupils, through 2200 local programmes.

DARE specially trains police officers to impart lifeskills and coach peer pressure reversal techniques, as well as the traditional giving of information, and reinforcement of society's attitudes towards drug abuse. An 80-hour training is given to selected experienced (i.e., not "rookie") officers. The officers make periodic visits in K-4th grade, to become a part of the school scenery. The main work comes in 5th or 6th grade, where fully 17 lessons are delivered (see Chapter 4).

Whilst in the British primary classroom it may not for some time be possible to involve police officers to the extent exemplified by the DARE programme, there is much that could be done. Using a mix of local beat officers and specially trained officers, primary prevention work could be effectively delivered in this key life stage.

Beyond this there are the same recommendations as for all the other communities, i.e. clean up your own backyard, visit other people's backyards and help them too, on duty or not.

## The Gentlepersons of the Press

There are more grounds for sympathy with the media than might be thought. They are to some extent only supplying what market research has indicated the public wants. A story of a huge drug bust or a dead addict is thought to sell more copies than coverage of a prevention event ... "Good News is No News" as they say. Hyperbole is the matchstick propping open the reader's eyelid ... "Small Earthquake in Chile, Not Many Dead" is the archetypal switch-off headline.

How then can journalists, of the level your prevention organisation is likely to work with, help you? The answer is they can help you greatly, and they will, once they understand the true potential of your work. Their problem at present, against a background of ever more commercialised local newspapers and of shrinking copy areas (to allow for even more advertising space), is that your story does not readily fit into their mental pigeonholes and repertoire of cliches for drug news. Addicts? No. Death? No. Arrests? No. Freaky Experiences? No. Sex and Violence? No. Hmm...

This means you have to spend time with journalists, to enlighten them to the possibilities of your work. Just sending releases in cold is low-impact action. Prepare the ground face-to-face, and in particular make it clear that:

(1) Prevention is the "**now**" thing, the real hope for solving this mess.

(2) They can get great copy and pictures from prevention events, on a **regular** basis.

(3) You are a pressure group (another pigeonhole) with the potential to improve many things in community life.

(4) They can be active, not just passive participants in the prevention process. They have an invaluable part to play.

(5) You know how to lay out and write copy they won't need to sub, and they'll get it when they expect it.

(6) You can and will give them copy, or instant quotes on any aspect of legal of illegal drug use. (Don't forget to say when you are "off the record"; it will be respected, on pain of your complaint to their Editor or the Press Council!)

Live up to these promises and you'll still be disappointed - sometimes. But the likelihood is that with time your reputation as a reliable newsworthy source will pay dividends.

Ask somebody like your local Civic Centre for a copy of their press list, which should include local freelances and "stringers" for the nationals. Now and again the latter may pick up on one of your stories. So also may local radio, hospital radio, and even regional/national TV if you can come up with a different news angle.

The Media Community, just like the others, has a backyard to keep clean, and could certainly join with other local community members, outside of duty hours, to work for a drug-free locality.

## Prayer Power

> "... Good physical health must be supported by mental or spiritual health (and vice versa for whole health)... we (also) need cultural or social good health... life from two basic aspects: the inseparability between physical and spiritual aspects of life (shiki shin funi); the inseparability between yourself and your environment (esho funi)... this is the wisdom of the Buddha."
>
> Kazuo Fuji, 1984
> "UK Express" Nichiren Shoshu (Buddhism) UK

> "The Hebrews didn't try to separate body, soul and spirit. All are of the same creation, and all have the same value before God. What we do with our bodies affects our spiritual lives. The reverse is true as well."
>
> John Throop, 1989
> "HIS" (IVCF/USA)

> "Prevent us, O Lord, in all our doings."
>
> Book of Common Prayer

These passages relate strongly to the non-religious-based Ancient Greek definition of "health" (given in Chapter 6 - "Health, what is it?"); in particular there is an uncanny similarity between Buddhist and Greek wisdom. Whether one is chanting Nam-Myoho-Renge-Kyo, or Our Father, or Allah Akbar, or affirming one's secular intent to be wholly healthy, there is a common thread in promoting one's own spirituality, the better to live one's life.

The religious communities in **your** community are therefore a powerful ally in primary prevention. They should be inherently committed to a drug-free lifestyle and able to promote it, not just from a moral standpoint (which may be valid for them but not for you) but also from the standpoint of spiritual and emotional health as a desirable aim.

On a more prosaic level, churches are full of "joiners", community activists who come complete with enthusiasm, skills, premises, resources (some), resourcefulness (lots), and a network covering both sacred and secular addresses. They are therefore an essential part of your network; one might say it would be a sin to leave them out.

It is quite likely that religious groups in your area, set within the British culture, can readily comprehend their relevance to and interaction with problem drug (including alcohol) users and those around them. For example, churches in many Thames Valley towns are, as part of their activities, acting as an outpost for Yeldall Manor rehabilitation centre near Reading. They will have more difficulty at first in understanding what they can offer to prevention. This myopia is understandable (forgiveness comes from another office). It is no different to the rest of society which operates, as Lofquist puts it, in a "symptom-focused" way. (See Chapter 6 - "The Real Prevention".) The answer for a religious body is actually more axiomatic than for someone outside it, and has been stated two paragraphs ago. To paraphrase Lofquist, we must get beyond the notion that prevention is only "stopping something happening" to a more positive approach that creates conditions that promote the well-being of people.

Some would call that Christianity. Or Buddhism. Or Islam. Or...

## Physician Heal Thyself

So much of this book has to do with health, and the scope for increased promotion of it, that we tend to overlook the need for introspection in the Health Community itself. Thousands of people work in and around this enormous service industry, and some are as much in need of help as the patients to whom they administer, directly or indirectly. American sources suggest more than 200,000 nurses in that country are victims of chemical dependency, and doctors would add significantly to this, not to mention auxiliary and administrative staff of all disciplines. The corresponding figures for Britain are anybody's guess, but there is certainly a need for help to those who may be too afraid or ashamed to ask for it. An understanding EAP would be a boon within the Health Service.

Moving from introspection to outreach, the health profession's members at all grades can obviously greatly help your community prevention plan. In America a related profession has stepped in; Pharmacists Against Drug Abuse is active not just in respect of misuse of pharmaceuticals but in prevention of all forms of drug abuse.

## Coalface Power

When a networking structure is drawn showing those disciplines engaged by a problem drug user, the following of "my drug use is my own business" becomes clear. Drug agencies, youth and community workers, probation officers, social service workers; all these and more are supplemented by voluntary groups of great variety.

Whilst these agencies are to a large degree at the symptom-focused end of the spectrum there are encouraging signs that many (with the perhaps obvious exception of such as probation workers) are prepared to resource primary prevention. Your encouragement of this welcome shift would do no harm. And even if the members of said disciplines in your areas are too overburdened with putting out the existing fires to have energy for preventing new ones, meetings between you and them should build mutual respect and the possibility of future co-operation.

## The Community at Large

This is going to be a short section, because most of it has been said already, in respect of other community sectors, or elsewhere in this book.

A few golden rules for community activists:

- Pace yourself. It may take years.

- Be a burnout prevention specialist.

- Identify where all the toes are, and don't tread on any.

- Ease yourself into the local scene; you may indeed be the Messiah, but look what the locals did to him.

- Plan your year with peaks and troughs, crescendoes and diminuendos. No one can maintain peak all the time, and media and public will get bored if there is only monotone.

- Be alert for process achievements and commend anyone in or near them.

One of the best, most detailed descriptions of community prevention to come onto the bookstands in the last few months is "Before it's too late" by Ernst Servais. Ernst heads up the Social-Psychological Centre in German-speaking Belgium. In 1979 the Centre drew up a 10-year plan around the assumption of a holistic approach; dealing with the needs of the whole person in relation to their whole environment (physical, psychological, social) through a whole-community response.

The 10-year plan had three phases:

(1) Create a working group within each target environment.
This alone took **7 years**.

(2) Co-ordinate these groups to derive a Central Co-ordination Team.

(3) Promote healthier lifestyles through drug prevention.

All drugs, legal and illegal, are addressed. From the outset the nexus between adult attitudes and youth behaviour was recognised; until adults had clarified their attitudes to their own drug use they would give mixed messages to the youth. (True, and worth making this valid point, but seasoned advice from the co-founder of PRIDE is:

> "Don't go in too heavy on this; studies show very little correlation between parent teetotalism or meagre drinking and child drug abuse. Greece has heavy parental smoking and drinking and yet one of the lowest incidences of adolescent drug abuse. Better to draw the link between abuse and immaturity, plus the need for awareness of self as well as one's children, rather than preaching and alienating the very people you seek to recruit. Once involved they will re-examine and reconcile their own behaviour with the programme objectives".)

The need to listen before you talk, to personalise prevention approaches after you have listened, and to take time in finding the right local organisers; these and other invaluable rubrics of community work were learnt. Technologies were tried and evaluated in classrooms, homes, workplaces, youth centres, leisure venues throughout the province. At the same time peoples' attitudes were being tested to identify correlates with drug use and drug avoidance. The point from Lloyd, Johnston and O'Malley's research (1986); that "attitudes precede behaviour by several years" was well taken. Approaches were developed to strengthen positive attitudes, as well as boosting self-esteem, opening up healthier alternatives including protest and risk-taking, and giving clear information on drug consequences.

**Does It Work?**

The results of twelve years hard labour in German-speaking Belgium are tainly encouraging. Since 1981 the beer-drinking and smoking habits of 14-18 year olds have clearly changed, with reduction of 21% and 10% respectively. Prevalence figures for illegal drugs were very low in 1981 (3% or less) and have not increased at all in 10 years despite great increases elsewhere. The usual difficulties with rigorous evaluation apply, but this small enclave of 70,000 souls, blessed with an experienced and vigorous prevention centre is better placed than many to provide good data. It will be interesting to see what effect there is, if any, from European border relaxation in 1992.

Parent training, pharmacist groups, media strategy, everything is in place. The year-by year subject attainment targets are somewhat behind what one would recommend for Britain, but this is a decision for each country based on its own culture and ongoing observation of youth psychological if not physical maturation. This is, however, criticism on a high level, and the mere fact that the book has been translated into four languages (French, German, Hungarian and English) gives some measure of its value. But see for yourself. Send for a copy.

* * * *

It is difficult, in a book providing an overview of the national and international approach to primary prevention, to do justice to any one aspect of an enormously complex and varied subject. The best that can be hoped for is that your appetite for community work has been whetted, for it is certain that without the community at large being involved your prevention will be, at best, patchy. However, in reading this far (unless you practice starting at the back of the book) your batteries should now be Long Life, enough for a long and fruitful run!

# EPILOGUE

This book has tried to provide the professional and the committed volunteer, of whatever discipline, with an up-to-date review of primary prevention technology, and some workable models for application in the British culture. This presentation started from the premise that primary prevention is necessary and desirable; feasible and viable. Hopefully, having read this far you too will agree that this is so. There are many pressures on our society, and particularly our youth, to resort to drugs. Some are ideological - liberty for youth, "legalise all pleasure" (this was a serious workshop resolution at a peer conference), validate users and encourage them to seek help by making drugs legal, and so on. More political aims may motivate some, but just as persuasive are simple curiosity, peer pressure, and the lure of risks.

Prevention will not cure unemployment, any more than it will design a better mousetrap. But it does have the undeniable potential to enrich and strengthen the lives of all those who experience it, and through its processes it could indeed improve society as a whole. Those in the prevention "manufacture and delivery" team, be they youth or adults, will themselves almost certainly benefit, however few other people they engage. But this "process achievement" would be a terrible waste of the promise that prevention holds. We can and must do better than this. Society at large needs to be informed, aware and in varying degrees involved. If the Strathclyde University research in 1991 proved anything it was that prevention means much more than education, and that throwing a few buckets of water on a fire may make the thrower feel useful but is unlikely to put out a major conflagration. Extending this metaphor to breaking point, the job of prevention workers may start with them acting as smoke alarms but more importantly it is concerned with producing an environment in which unwanted fires are at an irreducible minimum. (There will always be some.) The model for achieving this is, in effect, a synthesis of the second half of this book. Everything you do will help, and the more elements you have in place the better it gets. But beware Burnout, and keep in mind it took Ernst Servais in one compact Belgian community 7 years just to build an adequate network. And, most of all, remember:

**We rarely succeed at anything unless we have fun doing it.**

Have fun!

# APPENDIX A

## RELEVANT PUBLICATIONS, REFERENCES AND CONTACTS

### CHAPTER 1

**Nilson-Geibel, M** "Peer groups help prevent dependence among youth in the Federal Republic of Germany"
pub International Journal of Health Education (23), 1980.

**Sheldon, B.** "Behaviour Modification: Theory, Practice and Philosophy"
pub Tavistock, 1982, ISBN 0-42-77060-4.

### CHAPTER 2

**Bennet, W.J.** "Keynote speech" (including retrospective on Alcohol Prohibition). Pride Conference 1991, Orlando, Fla. Taped proceedings on request to PRIDE HQ Atlanta. See also "Prohibition 1920-1933; The Good, The Bad and The Ugly". Richard H. Schwarz M.D. Fairfax Hospital, Falls Church, Virginia 410, Maple Avenue West, Vienna, VA 22180.

**Bucholz-Kaiser, A.** "Legalisation initiatives in Switzerland" Unpublished report to PRIDE European delegates. 1989.

### CHAPTER 3

**NORML** "10th Anniversary" pub NORML, 1980. Gives details of International Cannabis Alliance for Reform.

**Peterson. R.E.** "Advanced Drug Legalisation Training" (Reading/Study Guide). Unpublished. Sponsored by PRIDE, 1991

**Trebach. A.S.** "Why we are losing the (Great Drug War) and radical proposals that could make America safe again".
pub Macmillan, New York, 1987. ISBN-0-02-619830-1.

**United Nations** "The UN Single Convention on Narcotic Drugs 1961 (as amended by 1972 protocol)" and "UN Convention on Psychotropic Substances, 1981". See also "UN Convention against Illicit Traffic in Narcotic Drugs & Psychotropic Substances, 1988".

**Wilkins. W.P.** "An appraisal of two mathematically-based papers related to drug abuse". Unpublished 1990.

## CHAPTER 4

**Cauchon D.** "Enduring high, low times" (story on High Times magazine) pub. "USA Today" newspaper 6 July 1990.

**I.A.P.L.** (International Anti-Prohibitionist League) Article in Boston Herald (Boston, Mass) 16 April 1990.

**INFNGO** (International Federation of NGOs for the Prevention of Drug & Substance Abuse) c/o Hong Kong Council for Social Service, GPO Box 474, Hong Kong.

**I.T.I.** (Illinois Teen Institute) I.A.D.D.A. 628 East Adams Street, Room 204, Springfield, Illinois 62701.

**Life Education Centres** (Mobile classrooms/trainings) P.O. Box 137, London, N10 3JJ (1992 Contact: Jill Pearman Tel: 071-267-2516)

**Lofquist W. A.** "Discovering the Meaning of Prevention" pub AYD Publications, Arizona, 1983 ISBN 0-913951-00-5.

**Malyon, T. (int. al)** "Big Deal : the Politics of the Illicit Drugs Business" pub Pluto Press, 1985. ISBN 0-7453-0008-1

**Masi. D.A.** "Designing Employee Assistance Programs" pub Amacom, 1984. ISBN 0-8144-5616-2

**Mersey Drugs Journal** "War - The Americans go over the Top" May/June 1988 issue. 10, Maryland St. Liverpool L1 9BX.

**National Curriculum Council** "Curriculum Guidance 5 (CG5) Health Education". pub NCC, 1990. ISBN 1-872676-23-5

**PRIDE** (Parents Resource Institute for Drug Education) The Hurt Building, Suite 210, 50, Hurt Plaza, Atlanta, Georgia, 30303, USA (Tel: 404-577-4500)

**Rose, Sharon** "National Red Ribbon Campaign" (National Federation of Parents for Drug-Free Youth). Apply to 1306, Oak Avenue, Davis, California 95616, USA.

**Servais. E.** "Before it's too late" pub Servais, 1991. Contact: Ernst Servais, SPZ-ASL, Schnellewindgasse 2, B-4700 Eupen, Belgium..

**Tribes** "A process for social development and co-operative learning" by Jeanne Gibbs. All information including UK trainings from PPP: 3, Radnor Way, Slough, Berkshire SL3 7LA

**Watt, T.** "Kangaroo Creek Gang" primary school video pack. All enquiries including UK training to PPP, 3 Radnor Way, Slough, Berkshire SL3 7LA.

**CHAPTER 5**

**Fast Forward** Contact office: Youth Clubs Scotland, Balfour House, 17 Bonnington Grove, Edinburgh EH6 4DP Scotland. (1992 contact Simon Jacquet Tel: 031-554-2561)

**Teenex** Contact Office: 3 Radnor Way, Slough, Berkshire, SL3 7LA, England (1992 contact: Ann Stoker, tel: 0753-542296)

**Youth Link** Contact Office: Ty Syriol, 49 St. Martins Road, Caerphilly, Mid Glamorgan CF8 1EG, Wales (1992 Contact Veronica Wilson Tel: 0222-885711)

**Youth to Youth** Contact office: CSSC (Catholic Social Service Conference) The Red House, Clonliffe College, Dublin 3, Eire. (1992 Contact: Chris Murphy - Tel: 010-353-1-360011)

**CHAPTER 6**

**Benard, B.** "Bonnie's Research Corner; Characteristics of Effective Prevention Programs". Derived from Illinois Teen Institute Adult Facilitator's Manual (Undated, obtained 1987). **Note:** All authors referred to in the section on Characteristics of Effective Prevention are called up in Bonnie's original paper. For more information on Illinois Teen Institute, contact Tony Renard, IADDA, 628 East Adams Street, Springfield, Illinois 62701, USA. Tel: 217-528-7335.

**OSAP** "Prevention Monograph - 3 : Prevention Research Findings : 1988" pub OSAP 1990 DHHS Pubn. No: (ADM) 89-1615

**CHAPTER 7**

**Blake R., Stephens E.** "Compulsions" pub Boxtree 1987 ISBN 1-85283-208-8

**National Curriculum Council** CG5 : ibid.

**Servais E.** (ibid)

## CHAPTER 8

**Benard, B.** "Peer Programs : The Lodestone to Prevention" pub in Prevention Plus II (ibid)

**Crime Concern** "Youth Crime Prevention Action Pack" pub 1991. Apply to Crime Concern, David Murray John Building, Brunel Centre, Swindon, SN1 1LY, Wiltshire.

**Greenspan, S.** "The Efficacy of Preventive Intervention : "A Glass Half Full?" pub Zero to Three (4), 1985.

**Kumpfer, K.** "Challenges to Prevention Programs in Schools : The Thousand Flowers Must Bloom" (from OSAP/Prevention Monogaph 3 - ibid)

**Moulton, O & C** "Guidelines for Evaluating Drug Prevention Material" pub Committees of Correspondence 1990. Apply to 57 Conant St., Rm 113 Danvers, Ma 01923, USA.

**OSAP** "Prevention Monograph - 3" ibid

**OSAP** "Prevention Plus" & Prevention Plus II" pub OSAP, DHHS Pubn. Nox. (ADM) 84-1256 (ADM) 89-1649 respectively

**Schaps, E.** (int. al) "Primary Prevention Evaluation Research: Review of 127 Impact Studies" pub Journal of Drug Issues (II) 1981.

**Sheldon, B.** "Social Work Effectiveness Experiments : Review and Implications" pub British Journal on Social Work (16) 1986.

**Swadi, H & Stoker, A.** "Adolescent Drug - Taking : Role of Family and Peers" pub Drug & Alcohol Dependence, 1988.

**Swadi, H. and Zeitlin, H.** "Peer Influence and Adolescent Substance Abuse: a Promising Side" pub British Journal of Addiction, 1988.

**Tobler, N.S.** "Meta-analysis of 143 adolescent drug prevention programs" pub Journal of Drug Issues 16 (4): 537-567, 1986.

## CHAPTER 9

**Stoker, A.** "Positive Health Promotion" (Working title). A model sequential curriculum for the prevention of negative behaviours, with special emphasis on drug and alcohol use, from Nursery to 18+. pub Positive Prevention Plus, 3 Radnor Way, Slough, Berkshire SL3 7LA.

## CHAPTER 11

**Berne, E. M.D.** "Games People Play" pub Penguin 1985 (21st reprint in UK) ISBN 0-14-002768-8.
**Faber, A. & Mazlish, E.** "How to talk so Kids will Listen & Listen so Kids will Talk" pub Avon Books, 1980 ISBN 0-380-57000-9

**Harris, T.A. M.D.** "I'm OK, You're OK" pub Pan 1975 (8th reprint in UK) ISBN 0-330-23543-3

**Perkins, W.M. & N** "Raising Drug Free Kids in a Drug Filled World" pub Harper & Row, 1986. ISBN 0-06-254811-5.

**Steiner, C, PhD** "Games Alcoholics Play" pub Ballantine 1990 (20th reprint in UK) ISBN 0-345-32383-1

## CHAPTER 12

**Johnston, L. & O'Malley, P.M.** "Why do the Nations Students use drugs and alcohol: self-reported reasons from nine national surveys". Journal of Drug Issues, Vol 16: 29-66, 1986.

**May, G.G., M.D.** "Addiction & Grace : Love and Spirituality in the Healing of Addictions" pub Harper Collins, 1988 ISBN 0-06-065537-2

**Nahas, G.G., M.D.** "Keep off the Grass"
pub Pergammon Press, 1979. ISBN 0-08-023780-0

**Pullinger, J.** "Chasing the Dragon" pub Hodder & Stoughton, 1987 (12th reprint) ISBN 0-340-25760-1

**Schuchard, M.M., Ph.D** "Teenage Drinking : Detour on the Road to Maturity"
pub. PRIDE 1986

**Schuchard, M.M., Ph.D.** "Parents Peers & Pot : Parents in Action"
pub US Dept. Health & Human Services, 1983, DHHS Pubn. No. (ADM) 83-1290

**Nahas, G.G., M.D.** "Marijuana - Deceptive Weed"
pub Raven Press 1975 ISBN 0-911216-39-1.

GENERAL NOTE: REFERENCES/INFORMATION

The Author welcomes enquiries regarding the above references, the references in Appendix B, or other aspects of this publication. Write to:

Positive Prevention Plus, 3,Radnor Way, Slough, Berkshire SL3 7LA

# APPENDIX B

# CANNABIS - THE INSIDIOUS GROWTH

Of all the currently illegal drugs, cannabis is the one that causes the most debate. There are many reasons for this. Despite the upsurge in use of "E", cannabis is still the "drug of choice" for many youths, most but not all them graduating from tobacco. As such, it is seen by some as socially preferable to alcohol...

> "I'd rather have somebody stoned on my arm than a drunk" (girl, Year 12). The option of an escort who was "clean" and sober didn't occur to her.

Another reason is that it is the drug of choice for some adults, who seek to justify their behaviour by pressing for societal approval in spite of the damaging implications for youth. The extreme limits of this interest group are populated by such as NORML and EMNDP, about which Chapter 3 says a little.

This leads to the third reason for seeking acceptance of cannabis; as a means to another end. That end may be the acceptance of more, or all illegal drugs. Or it may be a radical shift in society, using drugs as the lubrication.

Membership of all these three (and other) pressure groups is largely based on the premise that cannabis is relatively harmless. Adherents to this opinion range from 10-year-olds emulating older siblings all the way up to ostensibly learned bodies, such as the Institute for the Study of Drug Dependence (ISDD). "If cannabis is harmless, (it is argued) then criminal proceedings are an injustice and a waste of police and courts time". Further, if the stigma of illegality were to be removed then those users who are experiencing problems from this (harmless) substance would feel more ready to come forward and ask for help. "Anyway, everybody's doing it so it's daft keeping it illegal".

### The Acid Test

It is important that the definition of "harmlessness" used by the above pressure groups is clarified. It is in fact confined to **physical health criteria**. The other parameters of health, as defined already within the main body of this book, are not included. These parameters are:

- Emotional health
- Intellectual health
- Spiritual health
- Active role in community
- At one with one's environment.

Even if cannabis were to be proved physically harmless (and it is not), it would badly fail the test in respect of all these other parameters. Thus when ISDD say "there is no conclusive evidence that long term cannabis use causes physical dependence" there is no small degree of word-mincing going on. First, note that ISDD do admit that there **is** evidence, but it is not "conclusive". Conclusive for whom? And by what independent judges? And what does long-term mean... 3 years, or 30? Note particularly that psychological dependence is somehow overlooked, despite this being the source of severe social and personal problems with significant numbers of habitual cannabis users. The only certainty is that learned societies in **all** subjects (the author is a former chartered civil engineer) are jealous of their professional position and are resistant to admitting that previous theories may have been erroneous.

It is this reluctance to risk losing face (i.e. being blind to the possibility that acknowledging new facts may lead to new thinking, and will actually increase one's stature) that lies at the heart of the pro-cannabis body of opinion, lay members as well as professional. If you're a drug user you don't want to be forced to face the fact that you are risking your own future, and indirectly the future of those with whom you interact. Consider tobacco smoking in this context, and reflect on the attitudes expressed by smokers. Case proved.

**Death by Puff?**

Mention of tobacco brings to mind the old chestnut that "nobody ever died of smoking (or eating) cannabis". Two responses (amongst possible others) are offered:

> Solvent deaths have always included consequential accidents whilst stoned. The same should be true of cannabis. (Motor accidents have traditionally not incurred tests for cannabis.)
>
> Many people die every year of smoking-related illness. Tennant's research shows cannabis to produce cancer faster than tobacco, even though cannabis smokers use fewer joints than tobacco smokers use cigarettes. Most if not all patients presenting for treatment will be asked "Are you a smoker?" and are hardly likely to volunteer that it is an illegal substance they smoke.

Deaths resulting from cannabis ingestion, by even these two simple parameters are certainly more than zero!

## So Is It Physically Harmful?

There are reportedly 9,399 affirmative answers to that at the last count in the library of the University of Mississippi. All these papers testify to the physical dangers of cannabis. Presumably all 9,399 are deemed by the ISDD to be "inconclusive", and presumably the research references given below would receive a similar rebuke. You must make your own decision about this.

Three other sources of information are the books of Dr Gabriel Nahas, an internationally acknowledged authority on the subject of drugs. His book "Marijuana - Deceptive Weed" is a must for any serious student of the subject, whether you are "pro" or "anti". The second source is the Center for Brain Research in California; in particular Dr Robert Gilkeson. His video-based training pack "Myths and Marijuana" synthesises the findings of several leading scientists and researchers. A brief summary of the 90- minute film is:

> Cannabis does more organic brain damage than any other drug, with the possible exception of PCP and the end stages of alcoholism.
>
> Brain cell destruction has been observed even for "moderate" use, equivalent to one joint every other day for two or three years.
>
> Neurological function is impaired by the loss of even one cell, since cells are in chains of thousands of cells; one break and the chain is useless.
>
> The brain is the only part of the body having no pain receptors; brain cell damage is not therefore "noticed" in the way that a cut finger would be.
>
> Cannabis is much stronger now than in the 60s; up to 15 times as strong.
>
> Cannabis stays in the body for up to 4 months, so typical frequency of use means damaging cannabis molecules accumulate.

**Are You a Dope to do Dope? 'SPECT so**

The third and most recent information source, SPECT, is irrefutable. Whilst some desperate defenders of the virginity of cannabis struggle to dispute Dr Gilkeson's findings, on the grounds that some brain research relates to laboratory experiments on monkeys rather than humans, no such riposte can be levelled against Dr Sabeh Turner. Sabeh is the Director of Clinical Nuclear Medicine at Brigham Women's Hospital, Boston, Massachussets and he has developed a complex analytical and processing system, utilising brain scanners and state-of-the-art computer software. It is called SPECT, it takes brain slice scans and summates them to produce a colour three- dimensional 'photograph' of an actual brain. The photograph can be revolved to allow viewing from any angle.

Where any cell is dead there will be no blood flowing; the scanner therefore ignores this cell and it shows a 'hole'. Dr Turner's programme is still at an early stage but he has already been able to scan patients in a variety of conditions, and results with approximate ages (from memory when viewed by this author in 1991) included:

(1) 70 year old woman. Non smoker-drinker-drug user.
- Brain shown solid and rounded.

(2) 55 year old stroke patient.
- Whole of one side of the brain 'missing'.

(3) 65 year old male Alzheimer patient.
- Brain like Gruyere cheese. Holes everywhere.

(4) 35 year old heavy cocaine abuser.
- Brain same as for Alzheimer patient.

(5) **35 year old heavy cannabis abuser.**
**- Less damage than cocaine but still clear evidence of brain cell destruction.**

**Research Papers**

The following two lists give some indication of the vast amount of significant research available.

**RESEARCH ON CANNABIS EFFECTS**

Dr. Robert C. Gilkeson, teacher, paediatrician, adolescent neuropsychiatrist and brain researcher has conclusively demonstrated that the long term presence of the fat soluble molecules of cannabis decrease brain cell energy and lead to **more tissue destruction and long-term impairment of our highest intellectual functions than almost any other drug of abuse.**

Dr. Robert C. Gilkeson, The Centre for Drug Education and Brain Research, Venice, California.

**Marijuana increases risk of disease by inhibiting blood cells**
Study by Elizier Huberman, Director of Argonne National Laboratory University of **Chicago**. Study by Professor Marcel Bessis, Department of Cellular Pathology, **Paris** Medical School. Study by Dr. Cushman, St. Luke's Hospital, London.

**Effects of Ganja in farmers in Jamaica**
Emphysema, gastrointestinal problems, impotence, personality changes. Study by Dr. John Hall, Chief Physician, Kingston Hospital, **Jamaica**.

**Study by Dr. Forest S. Tennant, Director of University of California**
Drug Treatment Centre. Between 1968 to 1972 Dr. Tennent had examined lung tissue from French soldiers aged 19 - 24 smoking cannabis from 6 - 12 months. The lung lining tissues resembled those of nicotine smokers of 20 years duration and some showed pre-cancerous lesions.

**Mental illness**
Study by D. Zeidenbert - Associate Professor of Psychiatry, Columbia showed that 60% of mentally ill patients in **Morocco** used kif (cannabis).

**Marijuana can induce cellular damage when used on long-term basis**
Studies by: University of **Toronto**; Department of Cytogenetics, **Columbia**; University of **Utah**; **Swiss** Institute for Experimental Cancer Research.

**Marijuana may cause irreversible damage to the brain when used daily for 2/3 years**
Studies by: Dr. William Paton, Professor of Pharmacology, **Oxford** University

**Oxford University - International Consensus**
In 1974, 100 scientists held a 3-day international gathering - the subject was "The Pharmacology of Marijuana'. Sixty-seven papers were presented and the consensus of the meeting was:

> 'Marijuana is a drug with multifaceted action on nearly every body function: brain, heart, lung and endocrine. No scientist can refer to it as a "mild intoxicant".

There are many more scientific papers worldwide...
Dr. Kolodny and Professor Reese Jones, San Francisco
Dr. Soueif of Cairo

Professor Chopra from Calcutta
Dr. Costas Stefanis from Greece
Dr. Max Fink of the New York Medical Centre.
**and** the 9,399 papers in the University of Mississippi!

**RESEARCH CONCENTRATING ON CELL DAMAGE:**

**Dr. Gabriel Nahas, O.B.E., M.D., PhD.**
51 dope users aged 16 - 35, smoked 3 joints a week for 3 years.
3 out of 4 had discernible decrease in cellular mediated immunity (75% showed cellular impairment).

**Dr. Suciu-Foca, Oncologist and Jean Pierre Armand, University of Toulouse**
Lymphocytes from dope smokers compared to lymphocytes from non-smokers of dope showed dope smokers had lower lymphocyte response - lower cell division.

**Dr. Morton Stenchever, University of Utah, Professor of Obstetrics**
Lymphocytes of dope smokers show abnormally high number of chromosome breaks.

**Dr. Morishima, Professor of Cytogenetics, Columbia**
Dr. Morishima is concerned with cellular heredity - he found 30% of dope smokers' lymphocytes showed less than 46 pairs of chromosomes which indicates cellular deficiency (compared to 7 - 15% of non-dope smokers).

**Rudolph and Cecile Leuchtenberger, Department of Cytochemistry, Lausanne**
Cells taken from human lung tissue exposed to dope smoke had micronuclei with less than 46 chromosomes.

**Dr. Zimmerman, University of Toronto**
THC in very small amounts prevents the division of the single cell tertahymena (digestive tract).

**Dr. Julius Axelrod, (Nobel Laureate)**
The miotic index (% of cells in process of division) - 2.3% in dope users compared to 5.9% in non-users.

**Sir William Paton, University of Oxford, Professor of Pharmacology**
Found brain atrophy in young dope users equivalent to people aged 70 - 90 years of age.

**Dr. Wylie Hembree, Department of Obstetrics, University of Columbia**
Showed evidence linking heavy use of dope with impairment of gonadal function in men.

(Drs. Tennent, Patrick McGreer and Alexander Jacubovic showed cell damage in experiments in animals.)

**And In Conclusion**

Caffeine does not reduce lymphocyte function, aspirin requires 12 tablets daily to do so, alcohol even in large doses does not suppress lymphocyte functions. LSD never reaches high enough levels in tissues to do it.

**ONLY CANNABIS PRODUCES THIS KIND OF CELL DAMAGE - IT DEPRESSES, NOT SUPPRESSES CELL FUNCTION - HENCE THE DEBILITATING EFFECTS ARE ALMOST IMPERCEPTIBLY SLOW.**

# NOTES

# NOTES

## NOTES

# NOTES

# NOTES

# NOTES